CW01647943

Basic Function

The 4th Parachute Squadron, R.E. at Arnhem

`As usual, the men of the Parachute Royal Engineer Squadrons fought through to the end. Throughout the war we of the Parachute Regiment thought that it was almost a waste to use them as sappers when they were so good at killing the enemy. Shock troops in the full sublime sense of the words."

Major-General John Frost, CB, DSO, MC
from his book `A Drop Too Many'.

John Sliz

Copyright © 2010 John Sliz
All rights reserved. No part of this book my be reproduced, stored in a retrieval system, or transmitted in any form without the written permission of the author.

MGES-2 Basic Function: The 4th Parachute Squadron, Royal Engineers At Arnhem 1st Edition February 2010
ISBN 978-0-9783838-1-7
Editor-in-Chief: Laura Sliz
Editor: Thomas Shackleton
All Maps and Drawings by John Sliz

Front cover photos:
top: the remains of a PIAT position on the Graaf van Rechterenweg near the Oranjeweg. (Geert Maassen)
bottom: the culvert (John Sliz)
Back cover photo: the Ommershof after the battle (Geert Maassen)

Thank you to Geert Maassen, Cor Janse, and Philip Reinders for the use of the pictures and/or accounts and to Steve McLaughlin and Alistair Taylor for their help!

Other Books By The Same Author

The Storm Boat Kings: The 23rd RCE At Arnhem ***1944***
by Vanwell Publishing. www.vanwell.com

Engineer Assault Boats In Canadian Service
by Service Publications www.servicepub.com

The Wrong Side Of The River: The Polish Engineer Company At Arnhem

Assault Boats On The Waal: The 307th Engineer Battalion During Operation Market Garden

It is my best intention to honour the men of the 4th Parachute Squadron, R.E. by accurately recording their accomplishments. If you think that I have misquoted anyone, gotten anything wrong or have more information please let me know via my website.

visit: www.stormboatkings.ca

Contents

Maps

Drawings

Glossary

AA	Anti-aircraft
Abn	Airborne
ADS	Advanced Dressing Station
Bn.	Battalion
Bren	British machine gun.
Class 9	A designation for a bridge that can take loads up to and including 9 tons. ie, most medium trucks and cars
CO	Commanding officer
Comns	Communication
Coy	Company
Cpl.	Corporal
CRE	Commander Royal Engineers
Cwt	Hundredweight
Div	Division
DUKW	An amphibious truck
DZ	Drop zone
Est	Establish
FBE	Folding Boat Equipment mostly used for bridging, but was able to transport infantry
Fd Pk	Field Park
FOO	Field Observation Officer of the Royal Artillery.
GSO	General Staff Officer
HQ	Headquarters
Hrs	Hours
Indp	Independent
KOSB	Kings Own Scottish Borders. The 7th Bn was with 1st Airborne at Arnhem
L/Cpl	Lance Corporal
Lt	Lieutenant
LZ	Landing zone
MC	Military Cross
MG	Machine Gun
MM	Military Medal
MMG	Medium machine gun
MT	Motor Transport
NCO	Non-commissioned officer
O-Group	A meeting of commanders.
Op	Operation
O.R.	Other Ranks
PIAT	Projector, Infantry, Anti-tank
POW	Prisoner Of War
QM	Quarter-master
RAP	Regimental Aid Post
RAF	Royal Air Force
RAMC	Royal Army Medical Corps
Recce	Reconnaissance
RE/R.E.	Royal Engineers
RV	Rendezvous
Sapper	The equivalent to a Private in the Engineer Corps.
2i/c 2IC	Second in command
SP	Self-propelled gun
Spr	Sapper
SSM	Squadron Sergeant Major
USAAF	United States Army Air Force
Wrls	Wireless
X	Cross. Usually means crossroads

Introduction

This work is a snapshot of one of the engineer units that took part in Operation Market Garden, the 35,000 man airborne assault into The Netherlands to capture a series of bridges that would lead around the West Wall and into the heart of Germany. If all had gone well, Montgomery's 21st Army Group probably would have beaten the Russians to Berlin and ended the war before Christmas 1944. This epic battle has been told many times from an overall view and has been the subject of many debates of why the operation failed. This will not be repeated here. Instead, I offer a worm's eye view of a small specialized group of men who did everything that was asked of them and more; all with the bare amount of equipment and supplies.

Compiled from personal accounts, war diaries, reports and a selected bibliography, this is the story of the 4th Parachute Squadron, Royal Engineers (R.E.) during the nine days of Operation Market Garden. A story that in many respects mirrors the rest of the British 1st Airborne division yet, at the same time, is uniquely their own.

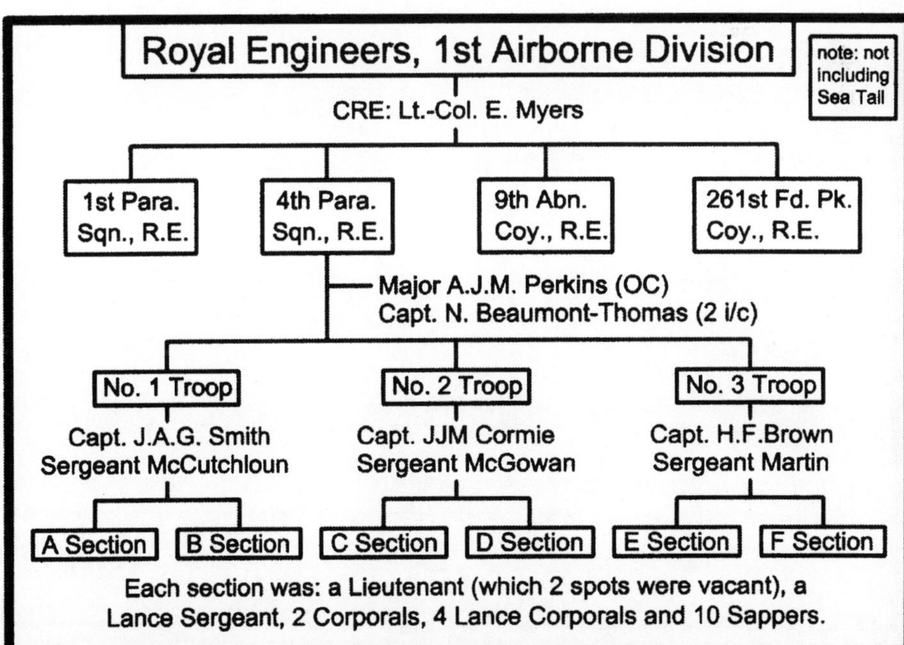

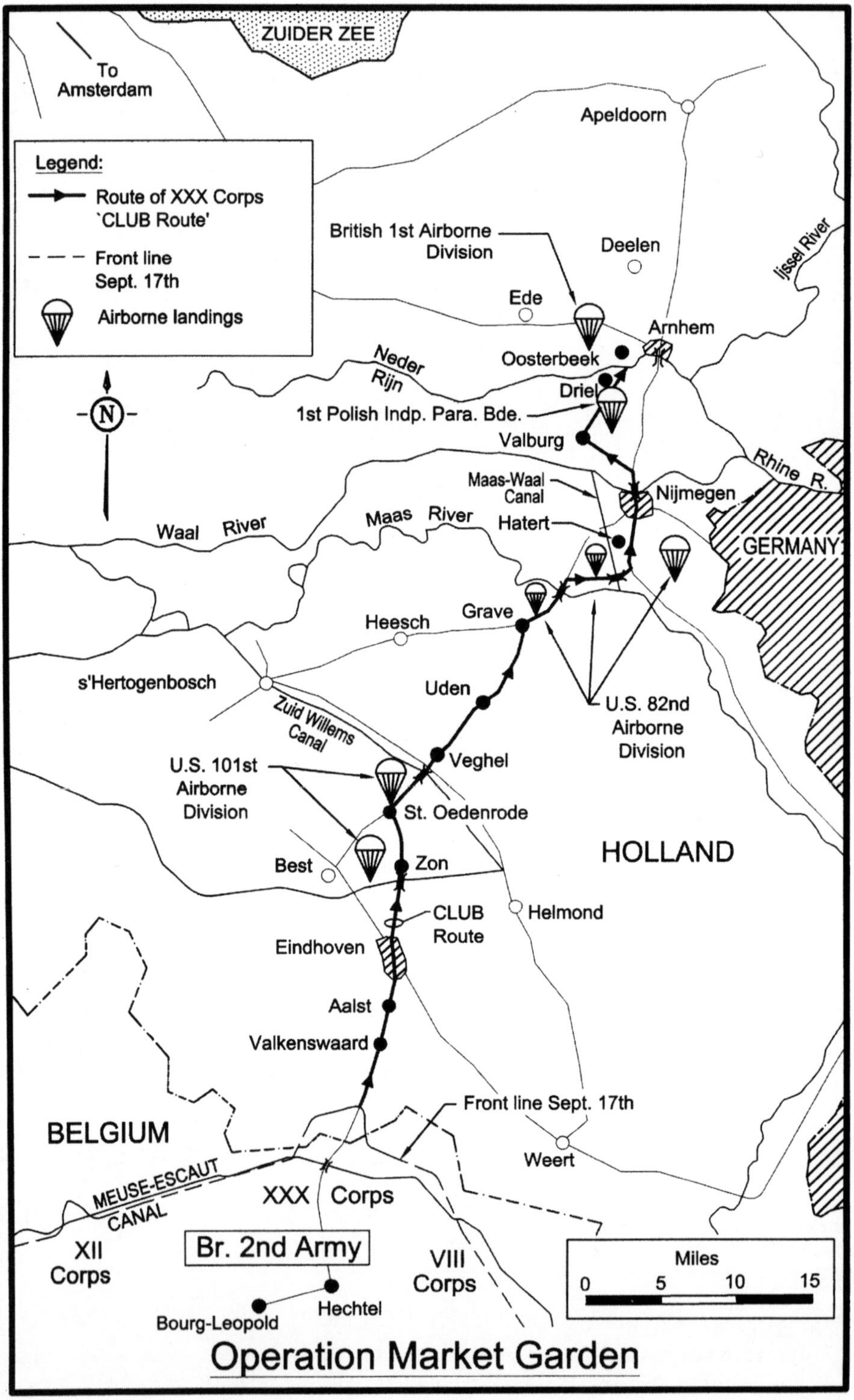
ZUIDER ZEE
To
Amsterdam
Apeldoorn
Legend:
Route of XXX Corps
`CLUB Route'
Front line
Sept. 17th
Airborne landings
British 1st Airborne
Division
Deelen
Ijssel River
Ede
Arnhem
Oosterbeek
Neder
Rijn
Driel
1st Polish Indp. Para. Bde.
Valburg
Rhine R.
Maas-Waal
Canal
Nijmegen
Waal River
Maas River
Hatert
GERMANY
Heesch
Grave
s'Hertogenbosch
Uden
U.S. 82nd
Airborne
Division
Zuid Willems
Canal
U.S. 101st
Airborne
Division
Veghel
St. Oedenrode
HOLLAND
Best
Zon
CLUB
Route
Helmond
Eindhoven
Aalst
Valkenswaard
Front line Sept. 17th
BELGIUM
Weert
MEUSE-ESCAUT
CANAL
XXX Corps
XII
Corps
Br. 2nd Army
VIII
Corps
Miles
0 5 10 15
Hechtel
Bourg-Leopold
Operation Market Garden

A Brief History

In December 1942 authorization was given to form `F' Parachute Squadron, R.E. in Moascar, Egypt from volunteers from units fighting in the Western Desert, and because the concept of airborne assault was still fairly new at the time its role was undefined and ambiguous. Its generic purpose was to support one of the newly formed airborne battalions in whatever role they were to eventually take on. At the time, the men were told that their primary function was to carry out acts of sabotage. To do this task, it was given a war establishment of 17 officers and 127 other ranks, but because of potential clandestine missions, in reality organization was based more on the Commando Troop* than the standard Field Troop, R.E. Each of their six sections had a Lance Sergeant, two Corporals, four Lance Corporals and ten sappers, of which two or three of them were drivers. Most of them were tradesmen such as blacksmiths, bricklayers, carpenters, joiners, draughtsman, fitters and electricians.

Eventually, `F' Parachute Squadron was assigned to the 4th Parachute Infantry Brigade and its name was changed to the 4th Parachute Squadron, R.E. The squadron served its parent unit in North Africa and Italy, and afterwards they sat in Britain for nine months waiting to get back into action. Many missions were planned and cancelled as the Allies advanced towards Germany.

At the time of Operation Market, the squadron had grown to 10 officers and 145 men and the Commanding Officer was Major Aeneas J.M. Perkins. He was a tall, athletic former officer of the Guards Armoured Division. His second in command was Captain Beaumont Thomas and his Intelligence Officer was Lieutenant G.S. Harris. Captain J.A.G. Smith led no. 1 Troop, with A and B sections under Lieutenants K.C. Evans and M.C. Eden. Both of these officers would have a different role during the landings. Captain J.J.M. Cormie led no. 2 Troop with C and D sections each under Lieutenant D. Millar and 2nd/Lt K.A. Hall. Lieutenant Millar would not take part in the landings. He was in charge of the Sea Tail and had to work his way up the corridor with the Second Army. Captain Harry F. Brown led no. 3 Troop with Lieutenant Thomas leading E Section and a vacancy in F Section. [1]

* A commando sub-section in 1943 was a Lance Sergeant, a Corporal, two Lance Corporals and 10 privates and this seems to be the order of battle for a section in a parachute squadron troop, though the paras had a higher number of NCOs.

Left: L/Cpl Maurice V. Weymonth
Far left: Captain H. Brown.
(P. Reinders)

The Mission And Equipment

A sapper can fight as infantry or he can perform field engineering tasks, and even though he cannot do both simultaneously, he must be prepared to do both. Therefore he must bring with him enough equipment to be able to perform either function. And there lies the problem as Captain Harry F. Brown, comments: *"A parachute sapper cannot take part in an airborne operation with anything like the equipment he needs. His roles are usually indefinite and fluid – he must be prepared for any eventuality, but especially prepared for his immediate task on landing."* [2]

To try to alleviate the lack of equipment problem for Operation Market, a number of men in each of the nine planes carried a kitbag with equipment such as: PIATs, Bren guns, wireless sets, ammunition and explosives. Also, every man carrying a rifle had either a pick or a shovel strapped to his felt valises. In addition to dropping the overloaded sappers, the planes also released containers with additional engineering equipment. Even more equipment was carried in the four gliders assigned to the squadron, one of them carrying a detachment of the engineers' equipment support company, the 261st Field Park Company, R.E. Still, it was not nearly enough equipment to cover every possible task, but it was hoped that this would be enough for the unit to be able to support the 4th Parachute Brigade onto its objectives. This was thought to be the use of flame-throwers, bangalore torpedoes and pole charges to help the infantry advance, then to assist them in preparing defenses by loop holing houses and creating road blocks. Once achieved, they were then to eventually relieve the 1st Parachute Squadron, R.E. of its road blocks into Arnhem from the north and northeast. Afterwards, with the arrival of the 1st Polish Para Brigade Group, the squadron - less one troop - would revert to the control of the CRE.[3]

Major Perkins had this to say on their pick of assignments: *"Unfortunately the best engineer tasks, which consisted, inter alia, of removing the charges from the bridges across the NEDER RIJN around ARNHEM had been allotted to 1 Para. Sqn. and a Det. 9 Fd. Coy. who were traveling in the 1st lift."* [4]

As well as the necessary equipment for their engineering tasks, the men of the squadron had to be able to defend themselves. Each troop was armed similarly to a standard infantry platoon, complete with Bren guns, PIATs and 2" mortars. Unbeknownst to them, they were going to need all of the weapons they had at their disposal, which if you asked the majority of the men at the time, would be fine. They had been waiting around in England for a long time and they were itching for a fight. Unfortunately, they got a bigger fight than they hoped for.

The Advance Party

On Sunday September 17th, an advance party from the squadron flew in a C-47 Dakota with chalk number 144. They were hitching a ride with the advance party from the 4th Parachute Brigade's headquarters as they went in with the first lift. Lieutenant Ken Evans' mission was to help the squadron's landing tomorrow by marking their rendezvous (RV) point on the drop zone (DZ). Helping him were Lance Corporal Jo Johanson and the Lieutenant's batman, Sapper Jimmy O'Donnell*. All three men landed safely carrying all the equipment that they could handle, including a 2" mortar with parachute flares to signal the RV. During the landing the next day, Captain H.F. Brown was to note the advantage of bringing the mortar. He said, *"The Squadron RV was clearly distinguishable because instead of using coloured smoke, Lt. Evans was firing coloured parachute mortar flares."* [5]

* Some accounts say that it was Sapper Sands and that would make more sense as he was in Evans' troop and O'Donnell was in Brown's troop. However, in Johanson's account he refers to him as O'Donnell, so I will go with that.

However, it wasn't as easy of a mission as it sounded as Jo Johanson describes: *"...at about 2:15pm, I jumped - rather fell, out of the door of our Dakota. The weight of the kitbag attached to my leg was too great to allow my exit to be classified as a jump. My chute opened and for a moment I surveyed the scene below me. Different coloured parachutes lay scattered about the dropping zone to the north, south, east and west. It reminded me of a crowded beach at Brighton. I could hear a little small arms fire in the surrounding woods, and now and then I heard the explosion of a hand grenade. I was relieved to notice that there were no Germans waiting for me, with fixed bayonets as I had pictured when I had allowed my imagination to run free on the preceding days. But it was time I got organized, released my kitbag and lowered it. Then I tried to make out where our RV lay; but the ground below me didn't seem to bear any resemblance to the photographs I had been studying the days before. I was still trying to work out where I was when I felt my kitbag touch down. A moment later I was on Dutch soil. I undid my kitbag and put my kit on. I looked around and saw O'Donnell. He looked a trifle dazed, so I went over to him to find out what his trouble was. The rope of his kitbag broke and he couldn't find his kitbag. Also he had had a rather heavy landing which had slightly stunned him. We looked round and found his kitbag. His kit was a bit squashed but it didn't look as if the impact had done much damage. He fitted his equipment and we set off towards a farmhouse where we saw Evans."*

The Lieutenant was amongst a bunch of Dutch people who were handing out cups of water. After a drink they met the rest of the brigade's advance party at the RV, where, O'Donnell asked Jo about the status of his rifle. Jo looked down the barrel, saw that it was definitely bent and advised him to throw it away and pick up the first weapon he found lying about. Lieutenant Evans overheard this and since he had two weapons, a pistol and a Sten gun, he gave O'Donnell his Sten. They left the DZ in single file and had not gone far when a Dutchman took Jo's photograph as he smiled and gave him the V sign.

Jo Johanson: *"One time we stopped by a children's school, the Germans had been using it as a billet and had to leave in a hurry, they had left a lot of kit behind. It seemed to me that this was going to be easy, I pictured our party walking to our brigade DZ and bedding down in our positions, and*

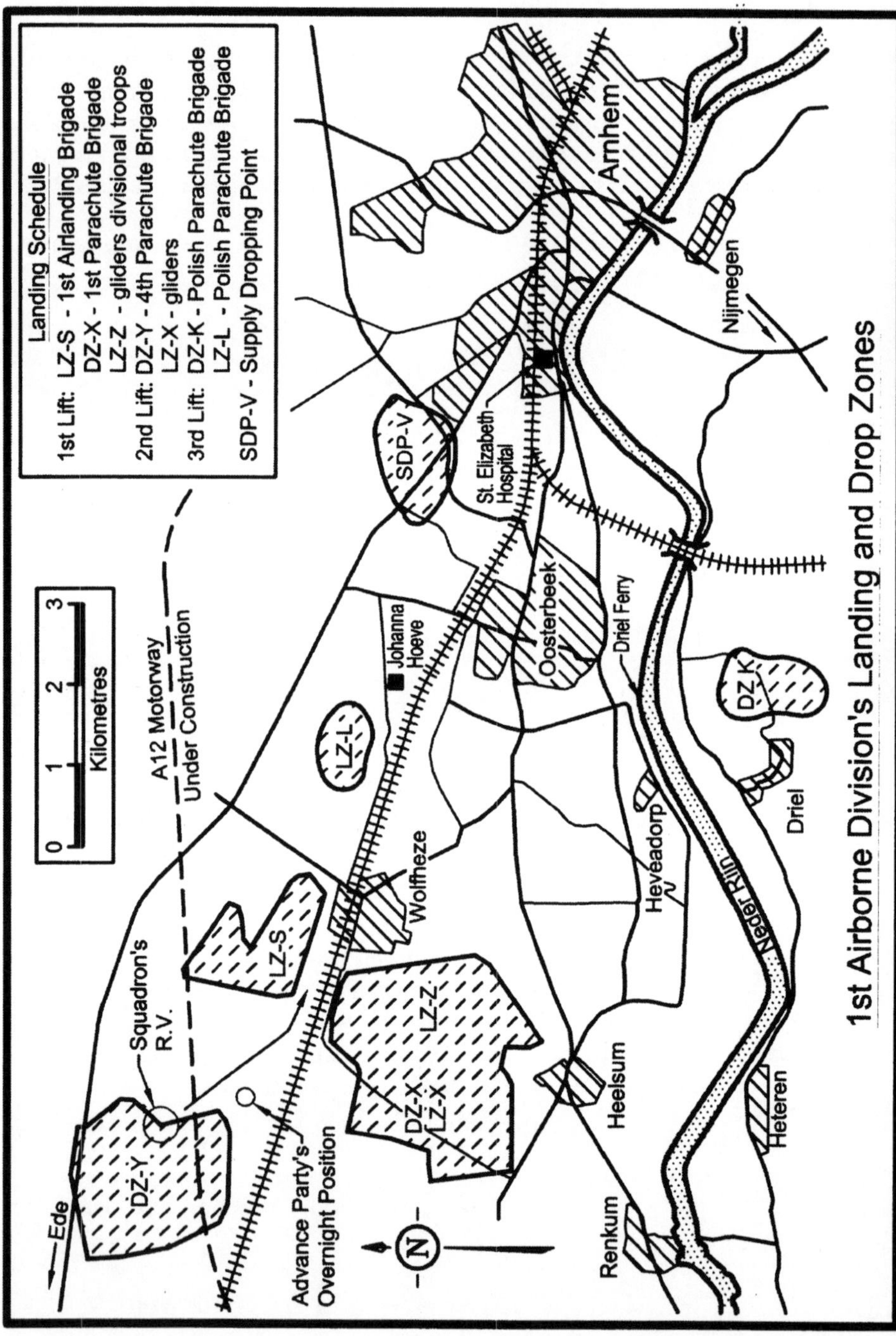

1st Airborne Division's Landing and Drop Zones

after all we were going to be relieved in 48 hours. When our brigade came down the next day, we would all march into Arnhem and perhaps the second army would be there by then." He was still daydreaming when a machine gun opened up in front of them, which rudely erased any possibility that his pleasant vision of the future would come true. *"I couldn't see what was happening, but I presumed our forward elements had bumped into the enemy."* They had run into the lead elements of the Dutch SS Battalion who they successfully ambushed. An hour later, they were on the move again and about a half a mile from the Ginkel Heath they dug in and were told to stop any enemy from coming through the woods. *"It wasn't a very pleasant night, it was pretty cold, and the wood was so dark that the enemy could have sneaked up within a few yards without being seen. Every now and then we would hear a small battle going on near us, but we were never called upon to fire."* [6]

What he did not know at the time was that the 4th Company of the SS Wach Battalion 3 from the Kampfgruppe Von Tettau, made up mostly of Dutch SS, was pushing from the west against the area where the 4th Para. Brigade was due to land at about 10 am the next morning. Fortunately, the Kings Own Scottish Borderers (KOSB), the battalion assigned to hold the landing zone until the 4th Brigade arrived, effectively dealt with the threat and the advance party had a peaceful night.[7]

The SS Wach Battalion 3 attacked shortly after sunrise on Monday September 18th and according to Jo Johanson: *"They were getting very close. I could hear the bullets whistling, and I could hear the Germans shouting to one another, but I couldn't see a thing in front of me except trees and bushes. At about 9:30 am platoon of KOSB went out and drove the enemy in our sector away, and for a bit we had some peace."* [8]

While Lieutenant Evans was waiting for the squadron to arrive, the Brigade Major of the 4th Brigade, Major B. Dawson, entrusted him a task that he wasn't exactly comfortable with. He was to become a reserve messenger in case the main messenger became a casualty. If something happened to Major Dawson then Lieutenant Evans was to meet Brigadier Hackett to tell him that: *"Things are not going to plan. Enemy in much greater strength than anticipated. Only 2 Parachute Battalion and elements are known to have reached the bridge. The General and Brigadier Lathbury have been missing some where in Arnhem for nearly twenty-four hours. Brigadier Hicks now in command of Division. The 4th Parachute Brigade is to detach the 11th Parachute Battalion which is ordered to proceed immediately into Arnhem by the south route. Brigadier Hackett is requested to contact division headquarters personally as soon as possible. Message ends."*

Lieutenant Evans was happily spared this task as the Major delivered it personally and later said, *"In retrospect I have often mused on the probable reaction of Brigadier Hackett if such a message had been delivered by a Lieutenant RE. As a renowned classicist historian, he might well have shot the messenger bringing bad news."* [9]

The advance party was ready to dash on the DZ to put up their signals and after awhile, *"...heard the drone of planes. We looked up and saw sev-*

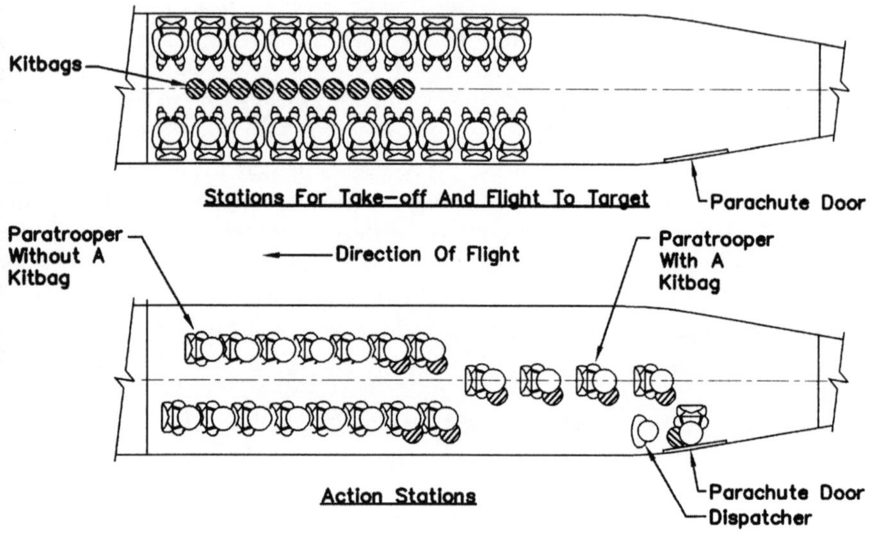

C–47 Troop Loading Diagrams

eral fighters flying fairly high. We thought this was the fighter escort, then they came down and started strafing some of our own troops. It was then we saw that they had black crosses painted on their wings." [10]

They watched twenty to thirty Messerschmitt 109s strafe the landing areas and this set some of the gliders on fire. This erased any belief that the Luftwaffe was finished. It also signalled that things were not going right and that this would probably take longer than the two or three days that was originally planned.

One of the problems was that the rest of the SS Wach Battalion 3 had been steadily advancing against the KOSB since late on the 17th and the rest of their battle group were on their way. Major Dawson thought that the enemy might try to by-pass the KOSB to the right and head towards Arnhem so he sent the advance party out on the right flank as a listening post. They went out about 150 yards along a path through the woods with orders not to fire, unless absolutely necessary.[11]

Jo Johanson expands on the Major's orders: *"He wanted us to watch till the enemy got pretty close and then crawl back with the information, we lay there for a long time, but the enemy seemed to be getting nearer. We still couldn't see them, soon we began to hear them shouting to one another, then we heard the crackle of the twigs under their feet and we heard them talking, and Evans decided that it was time we went back to report. A few minutes later we saw them crossing a path in the exact spot where we had just been lying."*

They were spotted and in the firefight, the Germans left two dead behind before disappearing back into the woods. The advance party had won this little battle, but generally things were not good. According to the original timetable, instead of fighting Germans they should have been guiding their squadron to the RV. The main reason for this was that the planes bringing in the second lift had been delayed for four hours, which left the men defending their DZ wondering what had happened to them. In the lull, rumours started circulating and one of them was that the enemy was forming up for a large counterattack with approximately 700 reinforcements. These did not seem to be untrue as, Jo Johanson continues: *"It started about 1.30 pm, we heard the rattle of MG's getting nearer, then some KOSB who had been on a patrol came back and told us they were coming and that there were no more of our men between us and Jerry. We heard the twigs cracking again and the German officers shouting orders. The bullets started whistling round my head, but I still couldn't see anything. An infantry sergeant on my right suddenly saw a movement and fired. It was getting very nasty indeed when suddenly there was a lull, everyone had stopped firing to listen, and there was an unmistakable drone of planes in the distance. The minutes dragged on, then someone shouted, "It's the 4th Brigade." We let out a cheer and when we saw the Dakotas through the trees, Evans said: "get our signaling kit and follow me."*

The planes of the second lift were also a signal for the infantry to put in a counter attack to clear the DZ. As the KOSB fought to regain Ginkel Heath, Lieutenant Evans led his party to the left hand side of the wood where a road ran up to the DZ. About two hundred yards ahead there was a highway under construction. The road they were on went through a tunnel under the highway. A short distance on the other side of this was the DZ where they could see the Dakotas unloading their men. The 4th Parachute Squadron's drop was timed to land twelve minutes after initial landing and their RV was the mid point down the eastern boundary, still a fair distance away. Jo Johanson: *"We just had time to double up to our RV and put up our signals, Evans led the way. I followed and O'Donnell brought up the rear. When we got to the line of the new road, some infantry were up on top of it firing at the enemy who were retreating into the woods. We went under the tunnel, Evans took the right hand side and I took the left. O'Donnell stayed in the middle rear. We emerged from the other side very cautiously, and at the same time the infantry came over the top. Evans started running forward again, our own troops were landing on our left but we knew that the enemy were still in the wood on our right, so we kept a good watch to the right as we made our way. I heard the crack of a revolver in the woods, and though I couldn't see anything I fired several rounds from my pistol in the direction of the noise. Evans also turned and let a burst from his sten. We had no time to stop, but we heard no more shots from that direction. We arrived at our RV and set off a parachute flare, our other signal would have been white smoke, but the DZ was all heather and Jerry had sent over some incendiary mortar bombs and as a result the DZ was a mass of white smoke. Two of our flares failed to function and no sappers turned up, so I went to see if I could find anyone. Men were wandering round the DZ looking for their kit and undoing containers. I was beginning* to wonder if the Squadron had been dropped on the right DZ when I heard a shout, *"Hello Jo! What's all the noise about?" I made some rather obvious remark about the enemy being somewhere near us. And went closer to see who it was."* [12]

Right Into A Fight

Backtracking in time a bit, the squadron was allotted one Vee-of-Vees formation of nine C-47s. Inside each aircraft were up to sixteen heavily laden sappers. Attached to each plane were six containers carrying everything from light weight motorcycles to grenades to Warsop drills. Major Perkins describes a special event on the fly-in: *"The men were all in great heart – singing and talking just as if we were off on an exercise. Some were chewing gum rather viciously. Suddenly there was a commotion at the forward end of the fuselage. The SSM had been sick much to the pleasure of the other troops. However all was well as he had used the paper bag provided by the thoughtful Air Force!"* This would have been the squadron's Sergeant Major, WOII E.S.J. Marriott who was sick.

All nine C-47's arrived over the north end of the DZ without loss and, amidst the heavy AA fire, released their passengers and containers. Major Aeneas Perkins describes his jump: *"Out went two folding bicycles and I followed. I heard my chute open with a crack and I was busy looking round to find my bearings. I could see our RV which was the corner of a wood at 632830 – nobody could mistake it. I felt confident that we should get nearly a 100% rally. There was a continuous sound of rifle fire and an occasional staccato burst of Bren or MMG. I hoped these sounds came from 7 KOSB, who had travelled in the 1st lift and were due to protect our DZ. By now I*

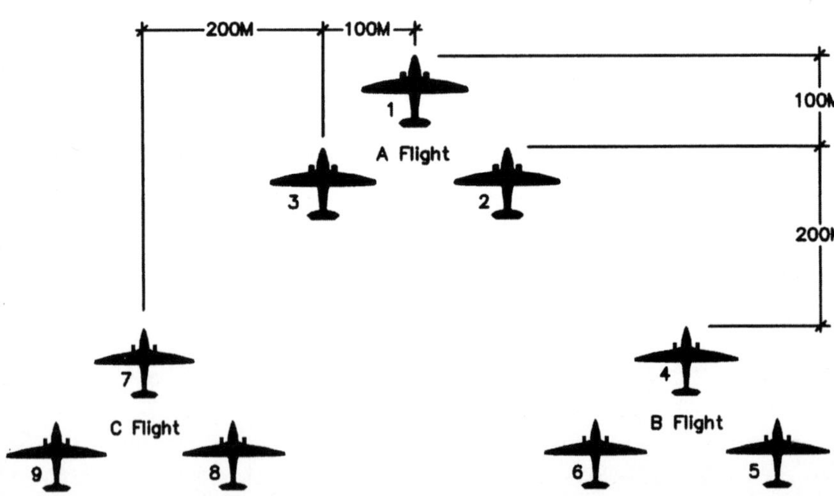

The Vee–of–Vees Formation
(Not To Scale)

had lowered my kitbag and glancing at the ground my rate of descent appeared to be very fast. I looked up at my parachute and saw the reason. My rigging lines were still badly twisted so I endeavoured to untwist them, but it was too late. I just managed to get my feet together as I hit the ground. This was at 1445 hrs. Something was wrong, I couldn't reach my release box with my right hand-in fact that arm was numb and useless. Thank God there wasn't much wind, otherwise I should have been badly dragged. After a few minutes I managed to release my kitbag and get out of my parachute harness with my left arm only. I got up, felt my shoulder which seemed to be in the most odd place; then I realized it was dislocated. I tried to get it back into place but it wouldn't budge. As I was transferring my web equipment, which felt like a ton, on to my left shoulder, Captain CORMIE 2 troop commander came up. We discussed the situation and I decided to make for 133 Field Ambulance." [13]

He was one of seven casualties upon landing. Sergeant McGowan broke his ankle, Sapper George Reid dislocated his shoulder, Sapper Bull had a bullet slice across his chin and Stan Holden received rope burn when he released his kit bag. Stan Holden describes his jump: *"As I lowered my bag containing equipment its weight made it fall very fast, so I made a grab at the attachment rope with my hand, causing a scorch mark across the palm. These kitbags were made to fit onto your leg with the bottom of the bag over the toe of your boots. You then had a line of about twenty feet which could be paid out. I was floating down nicely and able to have a good look around, listening to the snap and crackle of small arms fire. My landing was normal and I quickly had my equipment out of the kit bag and on my back, and linked up with the others of my troop. We were sent in the direction we had dropped, and came to a sandy track on the left towards the edge of the heath. We were met by Lieutenant Evans. I also saw a dead German lying on a bank by the track. I couldn't see any injury, so maybe he was just having a kip! I've no idea how he came to be so far inside our dropping zone. There was still a lot of small arms fire going on in the pinewoods surrounding the heath; though it had quieted a lot since the planes had lefts and things were fairly peaceful."* [14]

Corporals John B. Cooper and Reginald F. Taylor were reported killed in action on this day, but neither one of them have a known grave. Possibly, they were killed during the chaos of the landings and buried by the Germans who later failed to find their locations. However, some have reported seeing both of them later on during the battle, but these sightings have not been confirmed or denied.[15]

Captain H.F. Brown describes his almost non-eventful jump and landing. The only excitement was that, *"I almost landed on top of one of my sappers from another plane who was lying unconscious after a blackout from jumping."* [16]

W.C. Grantham remembers his flight and landing: *"Captain Nigel Thomas, MC was our stick commander. He stood in the open doorway of the plane and gave a running commentary on the countryside and location. I remember him with great pride. He was cool, efficient and confident. He was so relaxed and in command of himself – and us – that one would think that this was a regular occurrence for him. My landing was good and I gathered in my kitbag, which contained my PAIT gun, bombs etc."* It was then he realized that the DZ was under fire and quickly made his way to the squadron's RV. [17]

However, others were very aware of the raging battle going on underneath them. Sapper Weymouth was relieved that his chute opened soon after he exited the Dakota and was impatient to get on the ground a.s.a.p. *"We were very vulnerable coming in and we had been under fire even before we left the aircraft. I can still hear that peculiar `Thwack, thwack' sound as bullets passed through the fuselage and thinking to myself "Just my luck to start off with a bullet up the backside." Having made a somewhat heavy landing loaded with equipment, I found I had racked my ankle and had to hobble off the DZ to join my unit. Apart from rifle and machine gun fire aimed in our direction, parts of the heath had caught fire from exploding mortar and incendiaries. This all added to the excitement. After all, we were only here for two days, that's all we carried ammunition and food for."* [18]

At the RV, because the Major was injured, Captain Beaumont-Thomas temporarily took command of the squadron and recorded that the squadron was at 95% strength. One of his first orders was for a search for missing containers as only a few had been located so far.

Meanwhile, the three gliders carrying the squadron's motor transport of four jeeps landed - with varying results - on LZ-X along with the division's glider. One glider crashed into a ditch causing the tail to break off which smashed Sapper Ken Coley's foot and relegated him to the casualty clearing station for the rest of the operation. He eventually became a POW. The other two gliders landed safely and were unloaded.

At 1700 the squadron – now with the motor transportation from the gliders - moved off from the DZ and moved south to a new position astride the railway west of Wolfheze and dug in for the night. Stan Holden remembers: *"McIntosh and myself were ordered to dig in with the Bren facing away from Arnhem in the direction from which we had come. We scraped the stone ballast from between the two sets of rails to make a*

The destroyed flak train that the squadron passed. (Cor Janse)

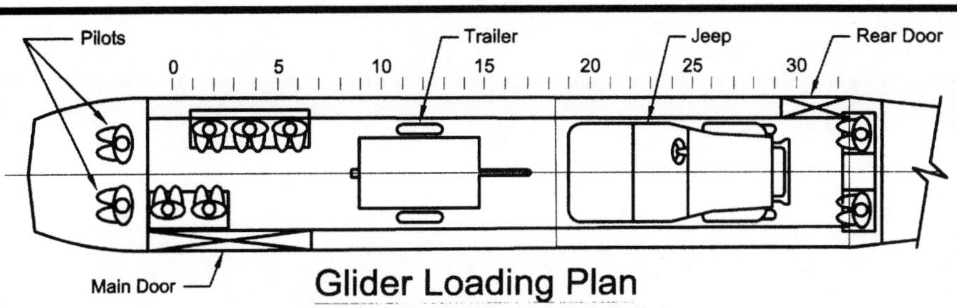

Glider Loading Plan
(showing max. loading for a jeep and a trailer)

slit trench. The rest of the troop was spaced out along the track and in the woods below the embankment. By now it was dark and we must have been the last people away from the DZ, hoping that Jerry would not be following us."

Soon after the 156 Battalion moved through the position and took no. 1 Troop with them as they moved down the line. Captain Smith's troop had a very difficult time keeping up with 156 Battalion, getting lost in the darkness and finding themselves east of Wolfheze and south of the railway lines. They eventually re-crossed the tracks and rejoined the battalion just in time to dig in for the night. L/Cpl. M.V. Weymouth wondered: *"Most of us who had been in action before wondered at the wisdom of calling a halt or the reason."* [19]

Just before daylight, on Tuesday September 19th the squadron was roused to `Stand to' until it was full daylight. Jo Johanson picks up the story as they moved along the tracks towards Wolfheze Station: *"We loaded all the heavy kit onto jeeps and trolleys, we also got hold of a four wheeled cart and hitched on to the back of Wheeler's jeep. When we got moving we must have looked like a circus. Every jeep was towing something, some men were walking some riding motorcycles, some riding pushbikes and the rest were perched on top of mountains of kit. The whole procession was moving at a steady fast pace of about 4 mph. I walked for a bit of the way till I saw an abandoned motorbike in a bush beside the track. I decided to try it out. With very little difficulty I got it going and it was a lot more comfortable than walking."* [20]

After he got a restful night's sleep, the medics cleared Major Perkins and by 0700 he was on his way to rejoin the squadron. As soon as he reached the level crossing at Wolfheze he was informed by an officer of the brigade staff that his squadron (less 1 Troop) was now the brigade reserve and they were on their way to take up positions at the crossing. The Major carried out a preliminary recce for troop positions and stood waiting for them at 0900 hours, noting that Wolfheze station and the immediate surrounding area showed the signs of bombing. The road and railway – including a destroyed German Flak train – had been hit hard by the USAAF a few days previously.

When the squadron arrived, they were put to work. Major Perkins: *"Defensive positions were occupied and I went off to see Brigade HQ, which*

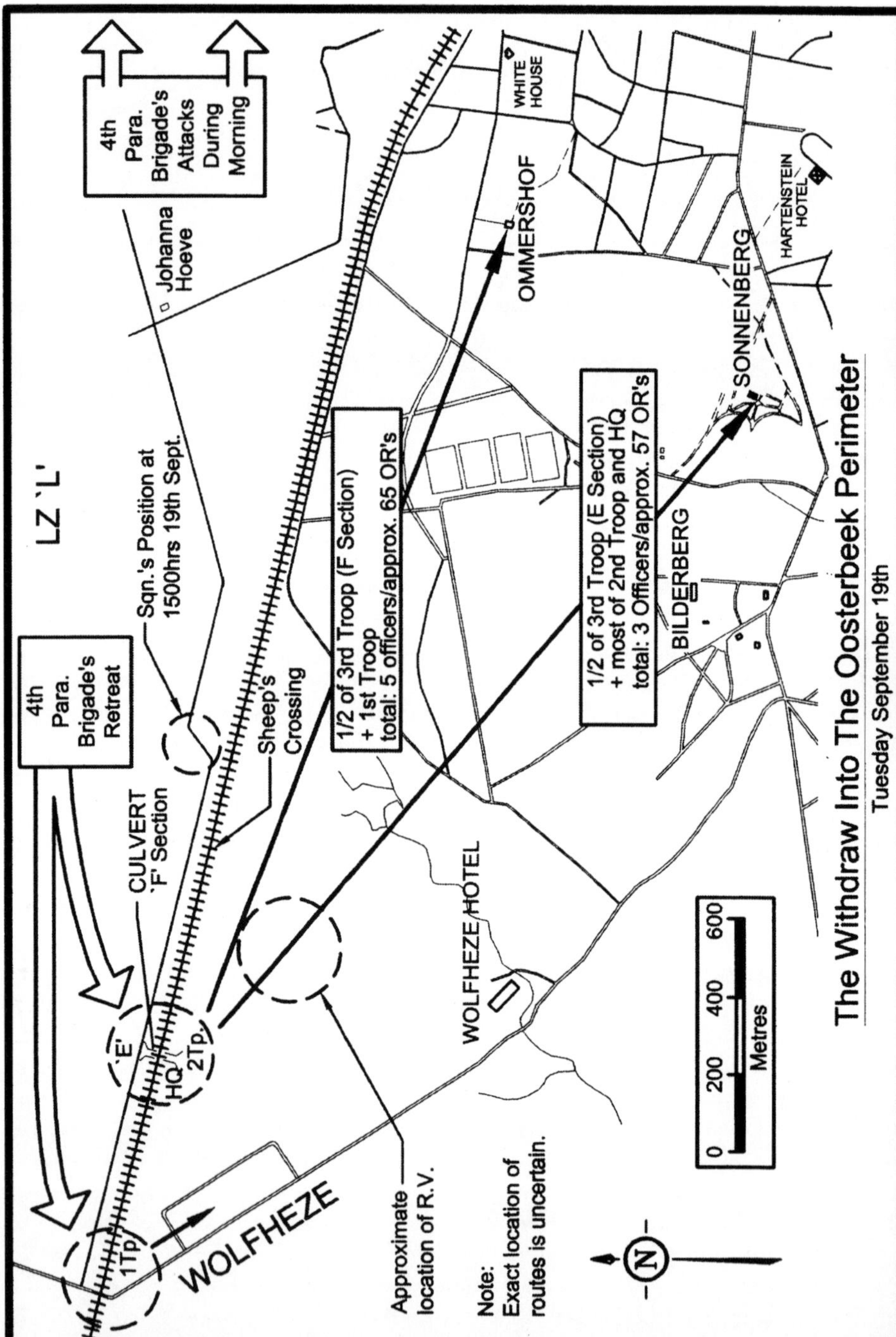
The Withdraw Into The Oosterbeek Perimeter
Tuesday September 19th
LZ 'L'
4th Para. Brigade's Attacks During Morning
4th Para. Brigade's Retreat
Johanna Hoeve
Sqn.'s Position at 1500hrs 19th Sept.
Sheep's Crossing
CULVERT 'F' Section
'E'
HQ
2Tp.
1Tp.
WOLFHEZE
WOLFHEZE HOTEL
Approximate location of R.V.
Note: Exact location of routes is uncertain.
1/2 of 3rd Troop (F Section) + 1st Troop total: 5 officers/approx. 65 OR's
1/2 of 3rd Troop (E Section) + most of 2nd Troop and HQ total: 3 Officers/approx. 57 OR's
OMMERSHOF
WHITE HOUSE
HARTENSTEIN HOTEL
SONNENBERG
BILDERBERG
0
200
400
600
Metres
N

was established in a house some 400 yards along the railway line towards Arnhem. During the morning we were strafed by some Me 109s, but these were out of range of small arms fire." [21]

Stan Holden also thinks that they were Me 109s. According to him, *"They came along the railway tracks at about 50 feet, so we smartly dived into bomb craters or behind some large tree trunks. The raid only lasted about 20 minutes and did not appear to hit anyone."* [22]

During this attack, Jo Johanson decided to try to strike back. *"I was in a bomb crater with Eric McCoy and we fired about three magazines. We watched the tracers going straight for the planes but as far as we tried we did no damage."* [23]

Fortunately, neither was there damage to members of the squadron and at 11:30 hours the men moved to the crossroads near the culvert and dug in. There they were strafed again. Stan Holden again: *"Since early morning we had been mixed up with various units and, with plenty of people around us, we seemed to have come to a halt. MacIntosh and I were told to take our Bren onto the open heath and dig in about 50 yards from the track. We started digging our trench slowly because, usually, no sooner had you got a slit trench dug and you had to move off. We were digging by a small tree, about six feet tall. Our trench was 18 inches deep: entrenching tools are not very good diggers in hard-packed soil. We heard the sound of planes, fighters, which appeared beyond the railway embankment and, sneakily, slowly cruising around in circles. Some people were saying they were ME 109s, others saying they were Spitfires: they were until they peeled off and started firing along the line of the track and the woods on the other side of the embankment. Somebody shouted not to waste ammunition firing at the planes. By now the track was deserted, with most people huddled in trenches or hidden amongst the trees. Mac and I felt very exposed. Now the planes circled around and came back firing up the valley at right angles to the track, right over our heads at approx. 50 feet, but it seemed a lot lower! The two of us dived into our trench and wished we had been more energetic and had dug deeper. It is a bit scary when you have a fighter plane giving you its individual attention. I think it only made two or three passes at us. I picked up one of its cannon shells and it was still hot. I think the fighters were aiming at the tunnel under the railway, which was full of people and wounded. We were called in from our lonely spot, a bit late I thought. Eventually the fighters went home and gave us a bit of peace. We were not yet on the move because there seemed to be a hold-up ahead, somewhere near the area called `Johannahoeve."* [24]

Up ahead the brigade was wasting away as it repeatedly attacked the strong German defenses set up along the Dreijenseweg, the road that ran north from Oosterbeek. The line is commonly referred to as The Spindler Line and was made up of first-class troops of the 9th SS Panzer Division. The 4th Parachute Brigade didn't know it at the time, but they weren't going any further. During the delay, W.C. Grantham was sent by Captain Smith to contact the leading company of 156 Battalion to find out exactly what was happening and to give them 1st Troop's exact location. He said,

*"Under fire I made contact with an officer of the battalion and passed on the message as instructed. I was then told that the attack on high ground had failed but there would be another attempt shortly, I had some difficulty proving who I was because, stupidly, I had forgotten the password. Whilst we were talking we came under fire from a sniper. I was then told to go and kill him because he was close to the squadron's position. I returned to my troop and gave the details of what I have been told. There was no more fire from the sniper so I wasn't required to go hunting (much to my relief). Later that day we withdrew under fire and covered part of the withdrawal by **156**. No-one I spoke to had any idea of what was happening."* [25]

During this time, Eric McCoy of the squadron's headquarters was sent to Wolfheze to obtain supplies of water. *"I left the jeep at the front of the house and began getting the water but when I came out the front door I was met by a number of Germans pointing their weapons at me. I ran back into the house and out of the back door and then headed back for our lines. As I ran along the bottom of the railway embankment the Germans ran along the top, they could have opened fire at any time and shot me but for some reason they didn't. Had they been SS men I'm sure they would have."* [26]

With the Germans closing in so quickly, it was an indication that things were really starting to go wrong. By now the drop zones had been or were about to be completely overrun and with their attack stopped to the east, the 4th Brigade was in danger of being surrounded. Also, the enemy were able to bring their AA guns well within range as the squadron helplessly watched the 1430 supply drop. Stan Holden: *"Anti-aircraft guns now started firing again and the sound of planes and small arms fire came from ahead. The planes were Dakotas bringing supplies. They first appeared coming from the direction of Wolfheze, a mile or so to our left. Again all sorts of gunfire was going on, similar to the day before but on a smaller scale. Viewed from the ground the sky in the distance seemed full of planes, and we had a grandstand view."* [27]

Along with the re-supply drop came the Polish glider landing on LZ `L' and since the squadron's position was at the edge of the field, it was no wonder the sky seemed to be filled with planes. It was!

Just prior to this, General Hackett, called an `O' Group and ordered the brigade to disengage and withdraw. Major Perkins comments, *"Disengaging in daylight is a tricky operation at the best of times, but in this case the difficulties were increased by the landing of the Polish glider element on LZ `L' 6880 at the same time. The squadron was ordered to assist the brigade transport across the railway line, and then to an RV under the protection of 7 KOSB at a point in the woods SOUTH EAST of WOLFHEZEN."* [28]

Captain Smith, *"We had landed on Monday and by late Tuesday **156** Battalion had been very badly beaten-up. The only reason that my troop of sappers was not wiped out along with them was sheer luck. Monday evening and Tuesday morning we trudged along behind the infantry who were making fairly good progress against some light resistance which they man-*

aged to overcome until late Tuesday morning when they ran into some German tanks of a Panzer Division which wasn't supposed to be there. They were taking a beating when Colonel Sir Richard DeVeaux sent for me and told me to take my troop back along the road we had just come to a railroad grade crossing about a mile back, and hold it as he thought his jeeps and light artillery could not get across the railroad embankment where they were." [29]

A prewar postcard of Wolfheze. (author's collection)

Near their present location, Major Perkins discovered a footpath leading up the embankment to the railway lines and a storm water tunnel under the railway tracks, a quarter of a mile east of Wolfheze. He positioned his squadron as follows: 1st Troop was at the level crossing in Wolfheze, 2nd Troop was defending the culvert's south side, with part of the HQ Troop defending the north side, E Section of the 3rd Troop was assisting part of the brigade transport through the tunnel and F Section was helping the 17 pounder guns over the railway line and embankment at the footpath. It was quickly realized the difficulty in trying to get jeeps and guns across the railway at the footpath and two of the large 17 pounder guns were taken over this way before it was realized that the tunnel was better suited for this task. However, at the culvert there was a huge traffic jam (one veteran compared it to Piccadilly Circus at its worse) and a large number of vehicles were abandoned until Major Perkins ordered them to the level crossing. Many vehicles were reacquired and got over that way.

When he arrived back in Wolfheze, Eric McCoy had a pleasant surprise. *"I went back to Wolfheze and to my amazement found my jeep still there and intact."*

Once the brigade transport was across the railway line, the Major went to the RV where only Captain Cormie's and half of 3 Troop under Lieutenant Thomas (roughly 60 men in all) were waiting. Meanwhile L/Corporal Alan Aldcroft and a group from headquarters troop were still guarding the north end of the culvert. He and Charlie Salmon were manning a Bren gun and they saw Germans crossing the open fields and heard tanks to the north of them. Deciding it was time to leave they ran through the culvert, found Lieutenant Harris and discovered that the rest of the squadron had already moved on. They did not get far in the woods when they were pinned down by heavy mortar fire. After a few hours they met up with Brigade headquarters. As they headed towards the rest of the division they ran into resistance. Lieutenant Harris was ordered by Major Dawson to take his men to deal with some Germans that were holding them up.[30]

Alan Aldcroft was one of them: *"They had machine guns on top of barricades of piled up logs firing across the tracks and roads. Lieutenant Harris was in front of us throwing grenades and he went down, I think he was wounded in the leg. Geoff Morrison was shot and killed, I saw the bullet pass right through him and out of his back, we couldn't get to him because of all the shooting. Driver Bower was wounded in the hand and Charlie Salmon was shot through the face, we put Charlie on top of a jeep trailer, bloody fools that we were! Charlie told us to get him off the trailer as the bullets were whistling everywhere, we lifted him off put him on the ground and gave him a shot of morphine before we left. Squadron Sergeant Major Marriott was with us and was wounded in the back of the neck, I put his arm around my shoulder and helped carry him as we were all taken prisoner."* [31]

Lieutenant George Harris was shot in the right arm and also received mortar shrapnel in the legs and back. He was taken prisoner and taken to a dressing station by the Germans. L/Cpl Charles E. Salmon eventually died in Apeldorn and Spr Geoffrey F.W. Morrison has no known grave.

The north end of the culvert. (taken by author)

Meanwhile at Wolfheze, Captain Smith never saw 156 battalion again and he and his troop were in danger of becoming prisoners themselves. *"By this time the noise of the battle had died down and after a couple of hours or so it became obvious that nothing more was coming back. It was a fairly quiet afternoon for us. There was a small signal house whose floor was several feet above the railroad so I could see for a couple of hundred yards down the track where a few German soldiers were crossing the rail lines every now and again. We took a few pot shots at them now and again but they didn't seem to be interested in attacking us and I didn't see any point in chasing them and possibly losing control of the crossing. With evening coming on and nothing more happening I decided to move out and rejoin the rest of the division. The only problem was I didn't know which road to take. I had had a most unfortunate incident happen early that morning. I had lost my map. Maps had been in very short supply, presumably because the whole operation had been laid on so quickly they simply were not as available as they should have been, and losing the only map we had in the whole troop was pretty serious. I had actually lost it to a senior officer that morning. He said he had lost most of his equipment during the drop and when I showed some reluctance to give it to him he pulled rank on me in a big way. I still think I was a bit chicken in giving in. We had a choice of two roads and fortunately we picked the right one, so that just as darkness came we rounded a bend and were told to halt and give the password of the day! I surprised the lads in my troop, who had somewhat naturally dropped in a handy ditch, by actually remembering the passwords! We were directed to a position and to dig in for the night. It was about then that I began to realize that things were getting serious. German tanks could be heard rattling along a road through the woods about a couple of hundred yards away."* [32]

Jo Johanson describes how he got separated from Captain Smith and the troop: *"We got on the road to Oosterbeek but the driver in the leading jeep wasn't sure of the way. Someone asked me to go up a side road on my motorbike to see if it was the right way. I hadn't gone far when I found another motorbike in the middle of the road riddled with bullets. I looked down at my motorbike and decided it was better as it was. When I got back to the others Captain Beaumont-Thomas had turned up and was showing the jeep drivers the right way to go. When he saw me he told me to stop with him in case he wanted messages taken anywhere. Captain Beaumont-Thomas seemed to be the only one who really knew what was happening and soon got everything organized. He told me the main trouble was that the enemy by chance had put in an attack through the woods just when our brigade was crossing the railway. It had rather taken us by surprise and had had a bit of difficulty in disengaging. Luckily, the enemy decided not to follow up his attack and we got into Oosterbeek without any more difficulty."* [33]

However, even though they were on the edge of the perimeter, they weren't in contact with the rest of the squadron. So Captain Thomas left Jo, Fox and Hearn to try to find the squadron. Unbeknownst to them, the squadron had followed the 7 KOSB as it moved towards the divisional area via crossroads near the Bilderberg Hotel. Before they reached the crossroads the KOSB were picked up by jeep and moved rapidly into the division area, leaving the engineers to fend for themselves. Major Perkins describes: *"We marched on down to the X rds, very much on the alert for enemy opposition, but no untoward incident occurred. By now it was getting dark and as we neared Div HQ at HARTENSTEIN 6978 I sent Lt. Thomas forward to contact the CRE in one of two remaining jeeps. Contact was est. and I was ordered to report in person at HQ RE. Here I learned that the other half of the Sqn under 2IC had already reported and were now in def posn around OMMERSHAL 693792 in support of 21 Indp. Para. Coy. CRE after consulting GSO 1 at Div HQ ordered my half of the Sqn to spend the night in the area SONNENBERG 687785 where the 9 FD Coy HQ, the DZ clearance party from 1 Para Sqn and some of the Fd Pk Sqn were already est."* [34]

They were placed between two companies of the Border Regiment, `C' on the Utrechtsweg and `A' to their north. Patrols were sent out as temporary defensive positions were selected. Half of the men rested as the others worked, while the major carried out his own recce as best as he could.

L/Cpl Maurice Weymouth tells this story: *"I was relieving the occupant of a slit trench, but unbeknown to me, he had just been hit by mortar fire and was lying in the bottom of the trench, face downwards. I fell in on him and found him dying with a massive wound in the back. In his last sec-*

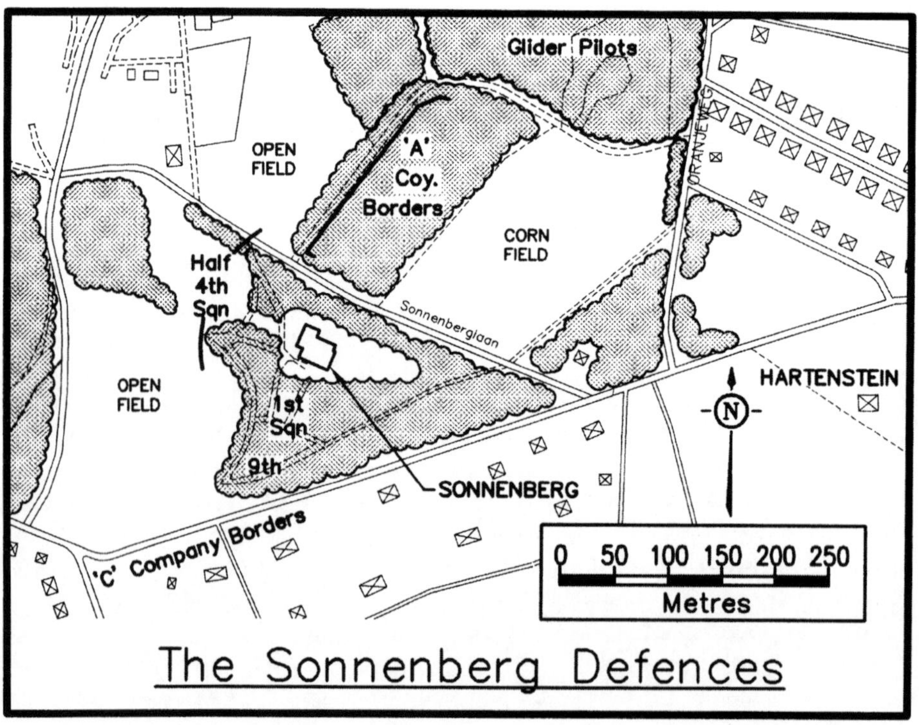

The Sonnenberg Defences

onds he was softly calling, `Mother, mother!' I didn't know the chap and, after the lull in the fighting he was moved away by stretcher-bearers." [35]

As the Major mentioned, half of the company was in position around a house called the Ommershof. This building was the holiday home of a Rotterdam shipping merchant and was north of Sonnenberg. This group was under the command of Captain Beaumont-Thomas. Lt Evans and his men resented being placed in front of the building. He claims that *"The Indp. Coy were on the high ground, in houses; we were out in front, in lower ground, just in holes in the ground – an attrition position protecting the Independent. Coy. The position had obviously already been occupied as weapon slits had been dug or partially dug. Whether we were under command of or in support of 21st Independent Company. I was never sure. At this stage we were five officers, Captain Beaumont-Thomas, Captain Brown, Captain Smith, Lieutenant Evans, Lieutenant Eden and about 65 O.R.s."* [36]

In reality, only the Independent Company's HQ was in the Ommershof. However, the sappers were placed in the most exposed corner of the sector with the pathfinders to their east and to their south.

The War Diary entry for 1800 hours recorded that Lieutenant G.S. Harris, SSM Marriott and 8 other ranks were missing. Also not accounted for was the attached party from the 261st Field Park Company consisting of Lieutenant W.H. Skinner and four other ranks. Unbeknownst to them, the Lieutenant, Sergeant-Major Marriott, Driver Bower and Charlie Salmon were wounded and captured, Geoff Morrison was killed and Lieutenant Skinner and his group were now prisoners.[37]

The sun lowered ending an all around bad day for not only the squadron, but for the division as well. They had been backed into a corner and it was only a matter of time before the Germans attacked. Men took turns keeping watch while the others tried to get some sleep. Jo Johanson remembers when it was his turn to keep watch for his isolated party. He heard tanks moving a short distance away and small arms coming from all directions. He realized then that they were completely surrounded. *"I thought how peculiar it was that only a few days before we had been back in a little English village with nothing to worry about. This was such an utter contrast."* Like many of the others, he wondered what had happened to the Second Army and worried that something had gone wrong. His next thoughts reflected the spirit of the division. *"Then I wondered how long we would be able to carry on, supposing the Second Army couldn't get to us. I thought how awful it would be if we ran out of ammunition and had to surrender. I thought of the headlines in all the German newspapers: "BRITISH 1ST AIRBORNE DIVISION WIPED OUT" – no, that was impossible, we could carry on for ever, we could capture German arms and ammunition. Anyway we could put up a good fight with bayonets. I laughed to myself as I imagined the squadron throwing bricks at Tiger Tanks."* [38]

Split

According to Montgomery's plan, the division was supposed to have been bolstered by Second Army by now. Instead, they were on their own and backed into a corner, which forced even the support elements to fight. As a result, on Wednesday September 20th, the squadron stood-to before daylight ready to defend their parts of the division's perimeter; a role that was normally meant for the infantry.

When it became light enough, the men at the Sonnenberg saw a few cows grazing at the far end of the open field to the west. As peaceful as the setting was, the open field grave them a good line of fire, which should mow down any attack.

During the morning light Major Perkins was able to study his surroundings more. He says that the *"...SONNENBERG was a large rather Victorian looking house, four stories high, and facing NORTH WEST. The house and various outbuildings had been used as a German soldiers billet. We found their remnants. There was a gap in the trees immediately in front of the house and it was possible to [command] most of the valley from the top storey. The wood on the right extended up along side a track to the NORTH WEST and the wood on the left which was only 100-200 yards in depth went down to the main road."*

These woods were held by `A' company of the Borders. One of their MMG teams was in position in the woods alongside the northwest track. The other R.E.'s main position was south of the house with a number of lookouts in the house. The Major felt that the house would soon become a target and a big one at that.

Stan Holden: *"Major Perkins came to inspect our positions during the morning. I was in our slit-trench trying to look busy. His shoulder was strapped up – he had dislocated it during the drop – but he looked reasonably happy! Anyway, he stood over me and said to dig in well as we would be stopping in this place for a couple of days. As squadron commanders don't often converse with lowly sappers, except when dishing out punishments, I felt privileged, and even dug out a few more entrenching tool's worth of soil from our slit-trench. But with so many tree roots it was hard work getting a good depth."* [39]

Meanwhile at the Ommershof, Captain Smith: *"Shortly after first light a German officer came out of the woods waving a white flag and a bunch of German soldiers sort of slid out from behind the trees. He said something about surrender and in my confused state I thought he wanted to surrender to us until one of my sappers, who must have had more sleep than I, pointed out to me that the Germans wanted us to surrender! I really didn't know what the right protocol was under these conditions, but since he was under the protection of a white flag I told him I would give him to the count of ten to get out of there. I shouted out ONE-TWO-THREE-and they started to disappear. And at the count of NINE- I dropped into my slit trench and then all hell let loose, - mostly I think from guys firing blindly at a bunch of trees! "* [40]

Still not part of the perimeter, Jo Johanson and his comrades went to a

Above: Looking west along the road on the north edge of the position at Sonnenberg. It was down this road that tanks came. The field to the right of the trees is the same field in the bottom photograph. (taken by author)

Below: The field of fire that the 4th Para. Sqn, R.E. and the Borders had. This is looking northwest from near the Sonnenberg. (taken by author)

nearby house and asked for a bucket of water. *"We had a good wash and the old lady in the house was very kind. She kept bringing out fruit for us to eat. Before we left I gave her ten Players. She was delighted. The Dutch hadn't tasted a good cigarette for years."* Tired of waiting, Jo Johanson decided to try to find Captain Beautmont-Thomas himself. Fox and Hearn came along as well. They made their way along a track and found Thomas

Field of Fire. Looking southwest from their position at the Sonnenberg. The house in the distance is near the Utretchsweg. (taken by Author)

coming the other way in a jeep. He told them to take the second right and then a left and go to a large house that looked like a castle. *"We took the second on the right and had gone a short distance when I saw a house that looked just like a castle. I decided that it must be the one and was making for it when Fox came alongside and stopped me. He called to my attention the fact that it was very lonely and there were none of our troops about. I looked around and decided to go back and find another house that looked like a castle. Eventually we found the right place and we were told the place we had been making for was full of Germans. We had been right out of our lines. I was lucky there were so many trees about, else we would have been seen and captured or killed."*

Jo brewed up some tea before he went into the building where he found Jock Standen surrounded by wireless sets. All of them had been damaged in some way and the two of them started working on repairing as many as possible. Also there were the Major and Sapper D.G.A. Coiden, making up the headquarters. Jo saw the Major for the first time since he had rejoined the squadron and thought that he looked pale. Still, *"I felt glad that we had a man of his caliber in charge."* The window of the room faced west towards the Germans and on the right was a pair of French doors that led to a verandah. The room had seen better

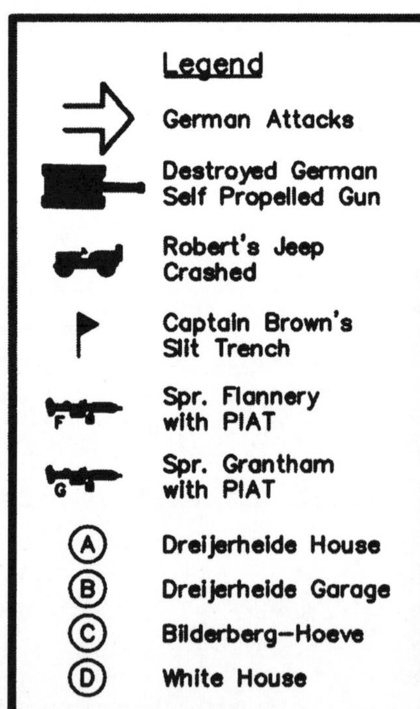

days as it was covered with pieces of brickwork, woodwork and broken glass.[41]

At the Ommershof the enemy was making its presence known. Two halftracks attacked, but were driven off by a few misses from a PIAT fired by Sapper Flannery. Almost immediately after the halftracks had left, a heavy mortar attack took the lives of sappers Leo Ackland, Richard Adderly and Frederick Yates. Also, fatally wounded was Captain Beaumont-Thomas. Ken Evans: *"A few yards further on I saw two bodies which had been moved to the inside of the track. The bodies of my two friends and comrades were lying on their backs side by side. Captain N. Beaumont-Thomas had been grievously wounded and was a bloody mess from the waist down his face was a rictus of agony. There followed one of the most traumatic periods of my life. I closed both men's eys and muttered a brief*

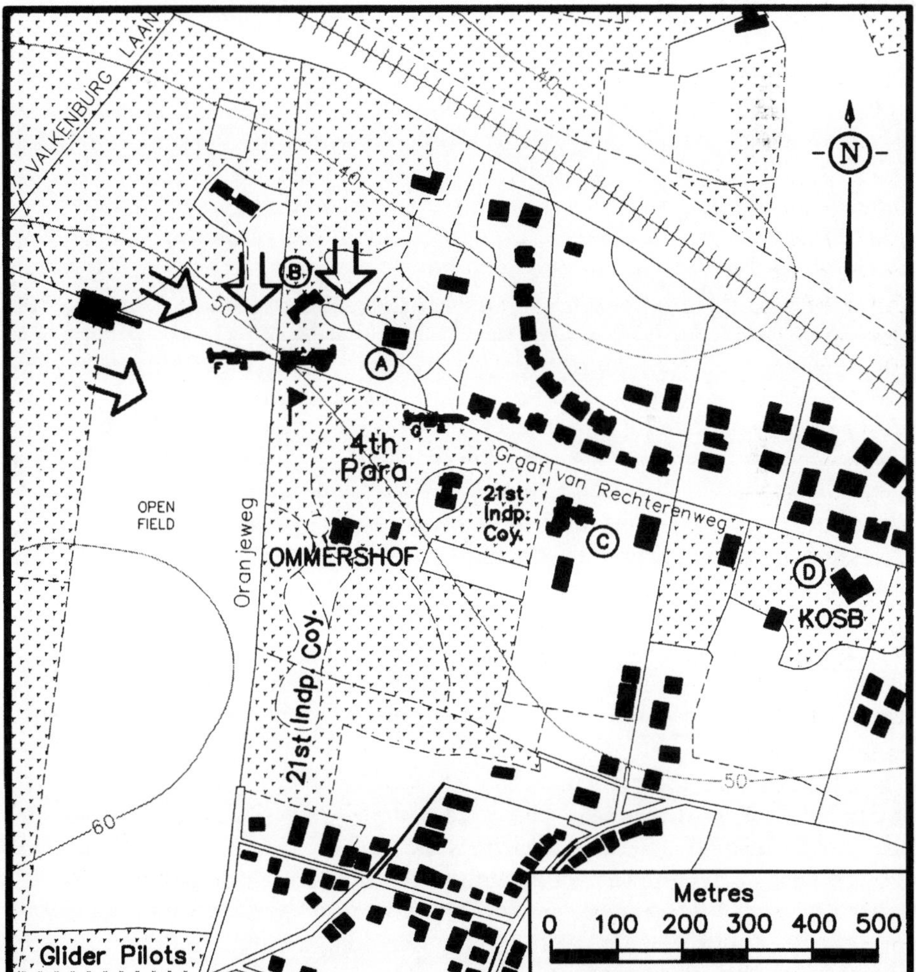

The Ommershof Position

and inadequate prayer. I endeavoured to control my involuntary retching (fortunately no food in my stomach so no vomiting). I then attempted to find and remove their personal possessions, placing them in sick bags from their smock pockets, including Captain Beaumont-Thomas' famous Zeiss binoculars. I asked one of the nearby men to find their gas-capes, which we carried in our large packs, and to cover the bodies. I then went off to find Captain Smith and Brown to pass on the bad news but when I found them they had already heard it." [42]

The news of the Captain's death quickly got back to the Major who said, *"A sapper arrived from the other half of the squadron at Ommershof bringing the sad news that the 2 i/c Captain Beaumont-Thomas had been mortally wounded by mortar fire and that Captain Brown had assumed command of that half of the squadron. I decided that it was essential to get reliable information concerning the situation there, so Lt. Thomas was dispatched in a jeep via HQ RE, to bring back a first hand report and est. wrls comns."* [43]

Lieutenant `Toby' Thomas and his batman Arthur Ayers left to contact HQ RE and Ommershof. They followed the Oranjeweg until it turned into a narrow track, which was bordered by a wood on one side and a field on the other. Ayers describes what happened, *"Suddenly several paratroopers appeared among the trees shouting and gesticulating to us, we took this as a greeting and waved back. Then without warning a hail of bullets came flying at us from the other side of the field, pinging on the side of the jeep and throwing up little clouds of dust as they hit the ground. Without any hesitation Lieutenant Thomas braked hard bringing the jeep to a shuddering halt and we both made an undignified dive out of the vehicle and dashed for the shelter of the trees. Without knowing it we had managed to travel into `no-man's land' between our forces and the enemy, how we managed to escape without a scratch I'll never know. When the enemy fire had died down we took a chance and with covering fire from the others we dived for the jeep. We shot off up the track with our heads well down as the Germans opened up again, we skidded at a sharp bend and narrowly missed a large tree. Lieutenant Thomas managed to regain control of the jeep and we missed the tree by inches, safely back on the track we continued our journey, by now out of range of the enemy gun fire."* They safely reached the Ommershof and were greeted by a German bullet that whined across hitting the bonnet of the jeep, forcing them to dive for cover again.[44]

As he awaited their return, the Major then set about organizing the squadron HQ in the house. His Intelligence Officer Lt. Harris had not been seen since the previous day and the food situation wasn't good, even though Corporal Tennant – the jumping QM – was endeavouring to take charge of such matters. All the water had to be carried from a house on the other side of the main road. Major Perkins, *"I made a tour around the SONNENBERG area and in the course of this est. contact with Major WINCHESTER, OC of 9 Fd. Coy. RE and Capt. GEORGE 2 IC 1 Para Sqn. After this I made for HQ RE to find out the general picture. I was*

Right: the Ommershof House photographed by G.R. Castendijk in 1943.

(from the Castendijk Collection, Gelders Archief at Arnhem)

Below: the Ommershof House after the battle.

(Geert Maassen)

anxious to concentrate the squadron in one location under my command, but CRE rightly decided that as both halves were finally dug in by now, it would be unwise to ask Div HQ for a move." [45]

At the Ommershof, the Germans sent in small probing attacks to determine where the British defenses were. Lt. Evans heard someone yell in German, *'Is that B company?'* Lt. Evans answered in German that it was, that there was no Allies near and that he should take a look. They did and were allowed to come within 50 yards before being cut down. Ken Evans:

The Ommershof was not the only house in the area affected by the fighting. Left top and above: the Bilderberg-Hoeve before and after. (Geert Maassen)

Middle: the Dreijerheide garage just north of the defences at the Ommershof.
Bottom: the Dreijerheide house was just north of Ommershof. Notice the building in the background. That is the garage where the driver lived. (Castendijk Collection, Gelders Archief at Arnhem)

"After the trauma of the earlier events I had no compunction in what appeared to have been a successful ruse de guerre, through whether my understanding of the apparent questions asked was correct, I shall never know. The consequences were certainly satisfying at the time. There was still the SP Gun and it was not long before the second bout of mortaring began. Clearly our position was not only exposed but fully pinpointed by the enemy." [46]

Shortly after the mortaring began, there was another attack. Ken Evans: *"During the afternoon we had General Urquhart who fell out of his jeep through our front during a concurrent visit from the enemy. In fact he came through about five yards from my position and I directed him up to the 21st Independent Company's HQ about 50 yards to our rear. General*

Above: the view in 1945 of the crossroads of Oranjeweg and Graaf van Rechterenweg looking north. (Geert Maassen)
Below: the remains of probably a burned out German vehicle near the same crossroads as the picture above. (Geert Maassen)

Urquhart later said that he found the 21st Indp. Coy. in good heart and very cheerful. Not surprising with half of 4th Para. Sqn protecting their position and taking the brunt of the battle." [47]

When the Major got back from his visit with the CRE, he discovered that Captain Cormie had rearranged the defenses in front of the Sonnenberg, a group of newly arrived glider pilots relieved the men in the woods to the south who had taken some casualties and Private M. Skelly (RAMC), the orderly attached from 133 Field Ambulance, was attending to the wounded in the cellars of the Sonnenberg. At his headquarters, Jo Johanson managed to get a few wireless sets going and one of the first things he did was to tune in the B.B.C. to see if he could get any news. *"The first*

Above: looking west across the field near the Ommershof. In the foreground are a fieldgrave and two canisters. (Geert Maassen)
Below right: shells left behind somewhere near the Oranjeweg. (Geert Maassen)
Below left: three supply canisters years later. (taken by author)

thing I heard was someone talking about the situation in Holland. It rather annoyed me. He was saying that now we had practically cut off the whole of Holland, it would be an easy matter to go straight through to Berlin. Perhaps if we had had the whole of Holland we could have gone on to Berlin, but it was all too obvious to me that we had not got the whole of Holland. Then he went on to say that the 1st Airborne Division north of the Lower Rhine were "surrounded but undismayed". I switched off and pon-

dered over the word "undismayed". It could have a variety of meanings." [48]

To the west of the Sonnenberg the enemy was spotted in front of a house on the other side of the field, but for some reason were not interested in attacking. Unbeknownst to the squadron, they were distracted by General Hackett and the remains of the 4th Brigade who still hadn't made it to the perimeter. Also, a flame-throwing tank had been sighted at the Utrechtsche and Valkenberg crossroads that inspired the relocation of the unit's few remaining PIATS to the woods adjoining the road, the Sonnenbeglaan. Like the infantry, the converted French Renault tank didn't come forward. It seemed to be waiting for something.

After a long journey, where they were again pinned on several occasions, Lieutenant Thomas and Arthur Ayers finally returned from Ommershof to report that the men were in great spirits, but short of food. The Major ordered that half the food be sent to them once it was dark.

Jo Johanson was lying on the floor tinkering with a wireless set when mortar bombs started falling more quickly than normal. *"One or two every few minutes was quite reasonable, but the rate now was about one a second and they were landing uncomfortably close. I took the wireless set I was working on into the corner of the room under a table and started tinkering again. Presently a small mongrel dog dashed into the room with his tail between his legs. He saw me in the corner and his tail wagged just a little, then he came up to me and snuggled up close to me. I stroked him and wondered what he was thinking about. All these bangs were beyond his comprehension, but he felt safer in my company."* [48]

Major Perkins describes what happens when company pops in unexpectantly. *"All No. 75 grenades had been collected from the men into a central dump with a view to putting down road blocks on the track road and the main road leading into our positions on the NORTH and SOUTH flanks respectively. I was in the process of setting the road block on the former, when there was a considerable noise of increased firing and suddenly through the woods to the NORTHWEST came the remnants of 4 Para Bde led by Brig. Hackett in person."* [49]

This was the end result of Hackett's charge with bayonets fixed from the hollow just west and into the perimeter. Seventy men were with the Brigadier. Major Perkins was hoping that some of his men were amongst them, but he was disappointed. *"From a conversation I had with the Brigadier on the terrace at the back of the house, it appeared that the Bde, which included our MT element, had been stationary during the previous night in the woods to the NORTHWEST of our position, and had been surrounded by the enemy. After a terrific battle all day a small party of personel but no vehicles had managed to break through to the Div perimeter. Unfortunately, none of the Sqn. MT personnel got out with this party, and we learned later that they were all captured or killed."* [49]

At 1600 hours, through heavy flak, Stirling bombers dropped supplies over the divisional area. Containers and panniers rained down on their position, some within immediate reach while others would have to wait until dark to be collected. A few hours later, Lt. Evans took a patrol north to the railway and from the top of the embankment saw eight Germans picking up containers from the RAF supply drop and using a copse of trees as a collecting dump. Annoyed by the large amount that they had collected so far, the Lieutenant ordered a quick fire from all present, including Lance Corporal Flannery with a Bren gun. A number of them dropped. They also saw about a company of enemy on the other side of the railway. They were preparing to attack. When Lieutenant Evans got back he reported the location of the collecting dump and was satisfied to hear the guns of the Royal Artillery were to try to take it out. Explosions were heard on the other side of the embankment.

At dusk Lieutenant Thomas and four sappers went out to collect the contents of the containers and panniers that could be reached. One of the party was Stan Holden. *"After stand-to at dusk we waited till it was pitch black then went creeping as quietly as we could to a pannier which we hoped would be filled with rations but was unfortunately filled with artillery shells, which are not very light! After much puffing and panting we managed to stagger with it back to the house where we put it on the veranda at the front, which was a bit silly really as a shell or mortar bomb would have set off the lot and made a mess of the house. The shells were taken away the next day as at the time were more important than food."*

Lieutenant `Toby' Thomas: *"We reached the containers when all hell opened up. The Germans had marked the positions and were waiting for us to collect them and had fixed line machine guns ready. I jumped into a nearby slit trench and heard a voice ask `Do you mind if I join you Sir'. It was Sapper Partridge who didn't wait for my reply but landed very forcibly on me. We eventually collected the containers hoping they contained food but they didn't."*

Sapper Eric Richards: *"I helped to recover several containers and panniers. One contained pajamas! Another blood plasma which we had no way to administer. Another contained a supply of loaded Bren magazines but when we tried to fire them they jammed every time, until we realized that for some reason they had been loaded with thirty bullets instead of the usual twenty-eight."* [51]

A second patrol was sent out from the Sonnenberg under Captain Cormie to determine the strength of the enemy facing them. Neither he nor the other four men with him made contact with the enemy. However, maybe that was a blessing because the 20th had already been very costly for the squadron. Six men had been killed and many more had been wounded and/or captured.

As usual `Stand-to' was at 0430 on Thursday September 21ST in preparation for a possible attack, which fortunately did not materialize. Afterwards, the Major and Jock Standon took a radio with them and set off in a jeep to visit the other half of his squadron at the Ommershof. The Major met with Major Wilson, the CO of the 21st Independent Para. Company who had nothing but good things to say about Captain Brown and the performance his men were putting up. Major Perkins: *"The men were in good form especially Lance Corporal Flannery who was using a PIAT with good effect. Some mortaring started up and we were forced to go to ground once or twice."*

Germans were heard and occasionally seen in the woods to the north, but due to the nature of the ground they could not be easily fired at. Still the sappers tried to get them. Major Perkins: *"Lieutenant Evans got behind a tree and started firing a Bren from the shoulder, and was about to throw some 36 grenades when I went up to join him; but a heavy burst of mortar fire sent us back to the cover of a slit trench. When this ceased, I glanced down in the trench to find a loaded 36 grenade with the striker pin released. I picked it up rather gingerly and threw it hard in the direction of the Germans, where it burst. I fancy the grease had not been properly removed around the striker pin, and this fact alone had saved us both."* Ken Evans says that the Major embarrassed him by making complimentary remarks. Major Perkins: *"However fate now turned against us – probably angry at our previous escape. As we were standing discussing our good luck, both EVAN's and I were wounded by mortar fire."* [51]

The major took a bad wound to the neck. Ken Evans: *"I thought he was a goner – myself in the left elbow and bad concussion."* The pair of them staggered into the house where Sapper Leonard attended to them. Then they were evacuated in the OC's jeep.[52]

At Sonnenberg Jo Johanson had waited for half an hour and tried for another half an hour to get the Major on the radio before giving up. He found out later that he was heard at the Ommershof, but for some reason they could not answer. Shortly after, a German officer approached carrying a white flag and was told in his own language what he could do with it and his request.

Captain Cormie took over command of the squadron as the Major and

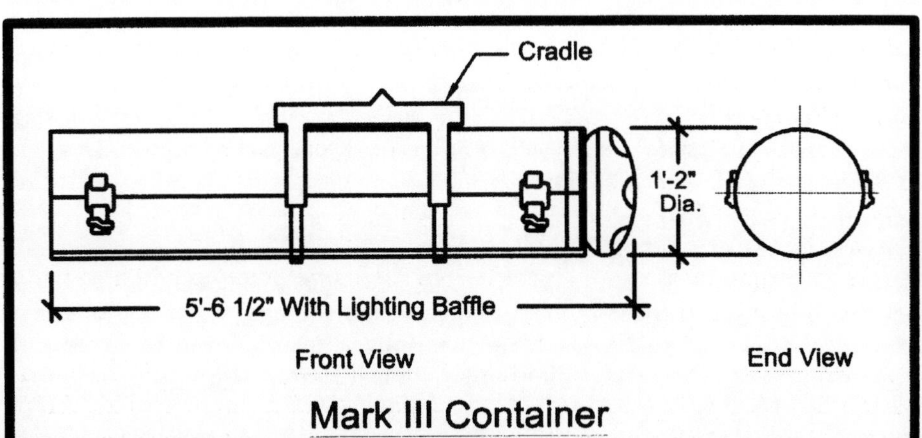

Lieutenant Evans made their way to the house where a RAP had been established. Then they were moved by jeep to Division Headquarters where the Major saw the CRE. Eventually, he and Lieutenant Evans were evacuated to an aid station where they stayed for the remainder of the battle and were eventually captured.

Later that afternoon men were seen gathering at the crossroads a hundred yards to the west. The War Diary states that it was an SP gun, but by Captain Brown's description, it doesn't sound like it was self-propelled in any way. Captain Brown said that *"It was impossible to identify them because of the trees, but it was clear that they were maneuvering a gun of some kind. L/Cpl. Flannery, our PIAT man, signaled to them with his celanese triangle and was met with a burst from a now very familiar Spandaus which actually chipped a piece out of the head of the bomb lying in his PIAT. He looked appealingly at me for a fire order and was told to keep firing until ordered to stop. The gun was now pumping rounds into our position from point blank range, but his fourth bomb silenced it."* [53]

With L/Cpl Flanney's last round, the crew of the gun fled, but they had done their damage. Lieutenant Eden took a piece of shrapnel to the back of the head and died instantly and three other ranks were wounded by the gun.

Around 1800 hours the shelling stopped and the sappers, who listened in disbelieving silence, heard a recording of "In The Mood". It was coming from the German positions. After it faded out, a very cultured German said in almost perfect English, *"Gentleman of the First Airborne Division, remember your wives and sweethearts at home..."* He was calling for their surrender. This was met with hoots, cat calls and whistles which drowned him out. It was clear from this spirited response from the men of the 1st Airborne that it was a big `No!' The enemy attacked again and approximately twenty of them fell before the attack was beaten off. But there was a cost.[54]

Stan Holden recalls: *"I think that it was on this day Driver Seabrook was so badly wounded that he was left to die. He had a fairly shallow trench in the open area inside our lines where he remained during the entire battle so far. Presumably he was killed by the shelling. I spoke to the medical corporal from the RAMC, who said he could not do anything for him. Incidentally, this orderly did a marvelous job, and seemed to be doing it all on his own. And all this took place in the cellar of the house, the only reasonably safe place around."* [55]

Around the same time, Coiden stepped out of the house for five seconds and was wounded in the head by mortar fire. Jock Shelly bandaged him up and took him to the temporary hospital. In the opinion of Jo Johanson he was the perfect medical orderly, who never got flustered or tired. And he wasn't the only one who thought so. Unfortunately, he was a very busy man. Also busy was Eric McCoy who made at least three trips in a jeep with wounded to the hospitals at the crossroads. He thought it was odd that the German snipers seemed to be firing at the jeep's tires and not at him. On the way back he was flagged down by two officers and told to take them somewhere. The officers climbed into the back of the jeep and they didn't get very far when a mortar shell struck the back. Eric was thrown forward and landed on the road unconscious. He was eventually picked up and taken care of by members of the 156 Battalion. He woke up in a cellar of a Dutch family filled with wounded.

Stan Holden, *"During one period of shelling, MacIntosh, Corporal Philip Hyatt and I hurriedly dove into a trench. When the shelling stopped we came up for a moment, and I received a hot blast in the face which blew open my eyelids. For a second I thought I had been blinded. After the shelling the Germans had sent over some mortar bombs which made no sound when coming down. One had hit the base of a tree as we rose out of the trench. MacIntosh, who was in the middle, said he had been hit and had a piece of shrapnel above his left eye. I had only got the blast. Blood was pouring down Mac's face from the cut over his eye. We put a shell dressing on the would and he dashed across to the house for attention. MacIntosh was blind in the eye and is fortunate that it wasn't a larger shell because that would have killed him."* [56]

Bill Grantham comments on the enemy: *"I occupied a slit trench in the middle of the road with my PIAT gun. In this area of the perimeter we withstood attack after attack and we fought with great fury. Armoured half -track vehicles and 88mm guns were used against us and I used the Piat to good effect. We didn't give an inch of ground and we shouted angrily at them to come and fight. There is no doubt that we unnerved them. We knew when they were going to attack because there was a lot of shouting and blowing of whistles, I think they needed a great deal of coaxing. In spite of many casualties we withstood everything they threw at us. It was fierce, bloody and noisy."* [57]

Arthur Ayers: *"Suddenly a hoarse voice shouted out `Here the bastards come boys, twelve o'clock in the woods' I looked towards the trees directly in front of me and saw about a dozen figures dressed in field-grey advancing towards us. They started to run, firing their automatic weapons and all hell let loose as our boys started to return their fire. I fired indiscriminately at the advancing enemy and saw several of them fall, not knowing if it was my bullets that had dropped them. I felt no remorse for my actions, no pity, they were the enemy and as such I had to try and kill them. They would have felt the same about me."* [58]

This attack, like the others, was repulsed.

The men had dropped with a supply of two 24 hour rations. By now most of the food had gone and stomachs were empty. During one lull in the fighting, Stan Holden went looking for food. During a trip through the Sonnenberg, he saw Sapper `Blondie' Nealon in the cellar at a long window set at ground level. He was sitting on a chair set on a table which made the right height for firing. The shelling started again and soon Stan Holden saw "Sapper `Lofty' Wheldon being carried away on a door. He had been wounded in the leg by a sniper and was laughing and joking about having a `Blighty' wound. His search for food was unsuccessful and after five days of waiting he wondered, *"Where the @#&! is Dempsey and his Second Army?"* [59]

To the east of the Ommershof and at the very tip of the perimeter, what was left of the KOSB was in a heavy battle for the White House and losing. Some of the KOSB withdrew into the squadron's area, bringing a valuable 6 pounder anti-tank gun manned by Poles with them. They counterattacked and regained the White House, but their numbers were so low that General Urquhart decided to tighten the defenses and give up the area that was of no major tactical importance. However that wasn't the only sector that was to be given up. The Ommershof was to be abandoned and the half of the squadron that was there and the 21st Independent Company was to be relocated. Bill Grantham: *"To my surprise we were told to withdraw from our position at Ommershof to an area close to the crossroads at Oosterbeek. We didn't know whether we were advancing or retreating. To those of us not in the know we began to realize that all was not well."* [60]

Unfortunately he was right. An "O" group by OC of 21st Independent Company informed them that the Div perimeter was contracting and that they were to report to Div HQ at midnight. Captain Brown and L/Cpl Dai Morris went to HQ 4 Para. Brigade where Brig. Hackett told them that there were less than a hundred men left in the brigade and that his men were the reserve. Captain Brown: *"Apparently things were not going well all around and we were ordered to withdraw to some kind of perimeter and I was ordered to have my troop form the protection of 4th Brigade HQ which was in some trees about two or three hundred yards from Div. HQ. This was four miles or so from the bridge...and that was as close as I got to the bridge."* [62]

The view today. Looking south from the corner of Graaf van Rechterenweg and Orjaneweg. (taken by author)

At 0130 on Friday September 22nd the detachment at the Ommershof moved into 4th Parachute Brigade's area. Before the sappers left, they buried Captain NB Thomas, Lt. MC Eden, Ackland and Adderly. Captain Brown figured that he had 2 Officers and approximately 35 men under his command. By 0400 the move was complete. They were now under the command of the 4th Parachute Brigade as their reserve or to be used by the CRE. They dug in defensive positions just east of the Hartenstein Hotel and just south of the hotel's stables. At first they came under intermittent mortar fire and endured constant shelling all day and it wasn't long before another man was wounded.

The cold wet weather, the twice daily mortaring barrage and the odd sniper did not make life pleasant for the members of the squadron. Bill Grantham: *"We dug in and envied the men who occupied the houses. Once again we were in open slit trenches, vulnerable to mortar fire, airburst and sniper fire. Near my slit trench lay a dead German. He drove a truck into our area and was killed. His truck was abandoned nearby. He began to smell badly so we decided to bury him in a shallow grave. He wore spectacles that fell off when we put him in the hole. We all agreed that we should put them back on his nose so that he could see where he was going."* [61]

Captain Smith: *"There was a small empty house next to our position and we used the basement for cooking. Cooking consisted of making some kind of stew from apples and some various kinds of turnips along with bits of leftover hard rations we could scrounge. We used to have little foraging parties go out under cover of darkness to root around in a nearby garden. Our numbers were gradually being reduced without us having anything to show for it as far as I could tell."* [62]

Around mid morning, Sergeant Mike Lewis of the press group showed up at the ruined stables with four members of the division. Mike Lewis photographed them as they moved through the ruined buildings, pretending to be on patrol. One of the photos that Mike Lewis took is probably the most famous of all images from Arnhem, even though it was staged. It shows the four men in the shot walking towards camera. All of this was within view of the squadron. In his book, `A Sapper At Arnhem', Harry Brown recalled: *"After everything we had been through we were rather disgusted at this untrue, artificial display of house clearance."* He also said that the sappers disapproved and let them know by catcalls and boos.[63]

At the Sonnenberg, a French Renault tank, which the Germans had converted to a flamethrower tank, attacked along the Sonnenberglaan and was driven off by sappers using Hawkins mines. Sapper W.A. Coulsting waited until the tank came close to his slit trench and then he pulled a string of 12 Hawkins Grenades across its path. For this he was recommended for an MM but received the Dutch Bronze Cross instead. At 1136, another tank was sighted using its flamethrower. Stan Holden: *"That morning the Germans attacked up the lane on the right (The Sonnenberglaan). It started with the clanking of a tank as it approached up the lane.*

This was further over to the right, therefore I could not see what was going on, but I fired into the trees lining the lane. The tank was stopped about 100 yards to the right and it seemed to be deep into our lines anyway. It was well and truly stopped by the Borders' PIATs I believe. It caught fire and blew up, its ammunition making a fine fireworks display. It was during this incident that Sapper `Jock' McKenna was wounded. He ran out of the house `to do battle', but was shot in his right hand. As he bent down to nurse it, he got a bullet in his arse – that stopped Jock's gallop" He was one of five casualties. [64]

The tank was knocked out by a 17 pounder gun positioned at the other end of the lane.

Then another attack came and Sapper Bromilow was the first to see them. He threw a grenade, but it went over their heads and landed behind them. This only drove them forward. Phil Andrew Hyatt – believing that it is better to be on the deck in these situations - apparently said, *"They're right among us"* then jumped out of his slit trench and ran towards a group of about four Germans who had gathered around a machine gun that had jammed. He hid behind a tree, pulled the pin on a grenade and then waited a couple of seconds. Then he lobbed it underhand where it exploded above their heads and killed three of them instantly. Phil Hyatt: *"I later went to search the Germans and one was still alive, the others didn't appear to have a mark on them and must have been killed by the concussion of the explosion. The one that was still alive gave me a tin of English cigarettes, he had a large wound on his leg so I tried to drag him back for medical help but he died before I could get him any. Someone else noticed that he also had a bad stomach wound, I personally found the Germans a most chivalrous opponent."* [65]

Meanwhile, the Bren guns were going flat out like they had been during all of the previous attacks. The men held their ground despite the mortar bombs bursting all around them sending dirt and hot lead everywhere. During all of this, Jo Johanson decided that the wireless situation was hopeless, so – with a pair of binoculars in hand – he went to the window and he spotted targets for Jack Leonard to shoot at. *"I would look out for a*

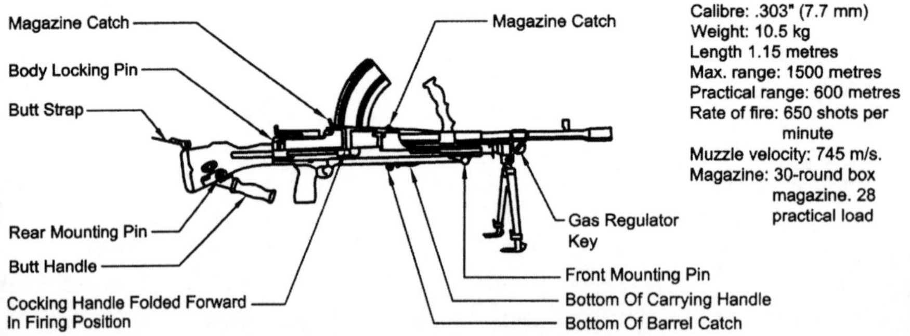

Bren Light Machine Gun Mk I

target and give him instructions where to shoot. Now and then we would swop over and he would do the spotting. We carried on like this for quite a long time, then we heard a M.G. open up on our left. From where we were we couldn't see where the bullets were coming from, so I dashed back into the room where I had been first, to see what I could see. I was standing beside the window, and I had just put the binoculars up to me eyes when there was a loud bang just behind me to the right. The blast knocked me over and when I got up my first thought was how lucky I was not hurt. I soon changed my opinion. Something in my left arm seemed to be trying to tear it apart. The whole of my arm was throbbing from wrist to shoulder and blood was trickling down my sleeve. Someone took me down into the basement, cut my sleeve away and put a field dressing on the wound, which was about two inches from my armpit. I lay down feeling utterly exhausted. If it hadn't been for the pain I could have fallen to sleep in a second. Shelly was out in one of the slit trenches treating someone else. After about ten minutes he came in and put a proper bandage on my arm and told me that a jeep would be along soon to take me away to a dressing station." [66]

Stan Holden was the number two man as Sapper Jock Patterson manned a Bren gun when the Germans attacked up the left side of the field towards the triangular copse. He said, *"There was a lot of shouting, as usual. As there were sappers in trenches inside the copse we were reluctant to start firing. I noticed a German had crawled up to the last of the trees in the copse. He lay behind a tree and attempted to throw a stick grenade. As he was so cramped it only came half way towards us. I tried to pull Jock down into the trench, but he was so busy firing that I don't think he noticed it. I was firing as fast as I could, but Jock told me to stop because I was deafening him. We had a bit of a row over it. Glancing to our left I noticed Corporal Phil Hyatt out of his trench with a grenade in each hand, his Sten slung round his neck. He was at the top of the path up which the Germans were advancing. This was only a quick glance as I was a bit busy to take much notice. However, he did eventually get a Military Medal for his actions. His citation said he stopped the Germans before they reached our positions, but in fact they did overrun some of our trenches. As the Germans retreated down the copse the sappers who were in the trenches*

A Bren Gun. (taken by author)

came out looking slightly pale. It had not been a nice experience. Things quietened down, which gave us time to clean our weapons. In England this had always been a bore, but now it was done at every opportunity, and in turns in case of surprises. Fear is a great slave driver!" [67]

Sapper Task

During the D-day drop, the 6th Airborne Division's Field Park Company brought 12 assault boats and 48 recon boats in by glider and were to prove useful. The decision not to bring in all of the 261st Field Park Company and its equipment was to prove costly to the 1st Airborne Division at Arnhem. Twelve assault boats and 48 reconnaissance boats would have been very useful in getting the Polish brigade across the river. Their three complete and fresh infantry battalions plus their support arms would have been very valuable reinforcements. For a division that was running out of men and ammo, reinforcements were vital and the plan was to get as many of them across the river as possible.

Major H.F. Brown, *"I went to see the CRE, and he gave me the job of transporting the Polish Parachute Brigade across the NEDER RIJN. All he could offer me by way of equipment was a few recce boats and some 10 cwt trailers. The night before his Field Engineer had tried to use an improvised `10 cwt trailer raft' without success. "We set off at dusk with fifteen men, six recce boats, one RAF dinghy, tracing tapes, signal wire and* a *FOO for communication with Division HQ. We reached the river at 698769, where the banks proved to be firm mud with stone groynes built out into the stream at about 100 yard intervals. Our plan was to attach signal cable fore and aft of the recce boats, and pull them across with two Polish paratroopers in each, then pull them back empty. The river was so wide and fast that the signal cable broke, and we had to resort to rowing one Pole across at a time. Two boats were punctured in reducing the total number to four recce boats and one RAF dinghy. Before the sappers started, they were all almost asleep on their feet and very hungry. One or two automatic weapons were firing just over our heads and an odd mortar bomb disturbed the otherwise swift, unruffled river."* [68]

Lieutenant Storrs and nine other sappers from another unit were also present. It took roughly twenty minutes for a round trip, even with the athletic Lieutenant Storrs (The Field Engineer) and Sergeant Juhas of the Polish engineer company. Lance Corporal Brown and a crew of three took the RAF dinghy, but it proved to be too difficult to handle and they drifted downstream for about two miles, way behind the division's control. Fortunately, they all found their way back into the perimeter.

By daylight only 52 men had been ferried across. Captain Brown felt bad about the lack of success and in his memoir `A Sapper At Arnhem' written 60 years later, beats himself up for it. Since the site was exposed and under direct fire, they had to return to Div. HQ as soon as the sun started to come up. Lance Corporal Flannery was left on the far bank, but as the others headed back the Captain waited for him to be rowed back across. The three of them had to sprint while lugging a recce boat for the best part of a quarter of a mile across the ponders. Exhausted, the three of them made their way back to HQ through heavy mortaring.

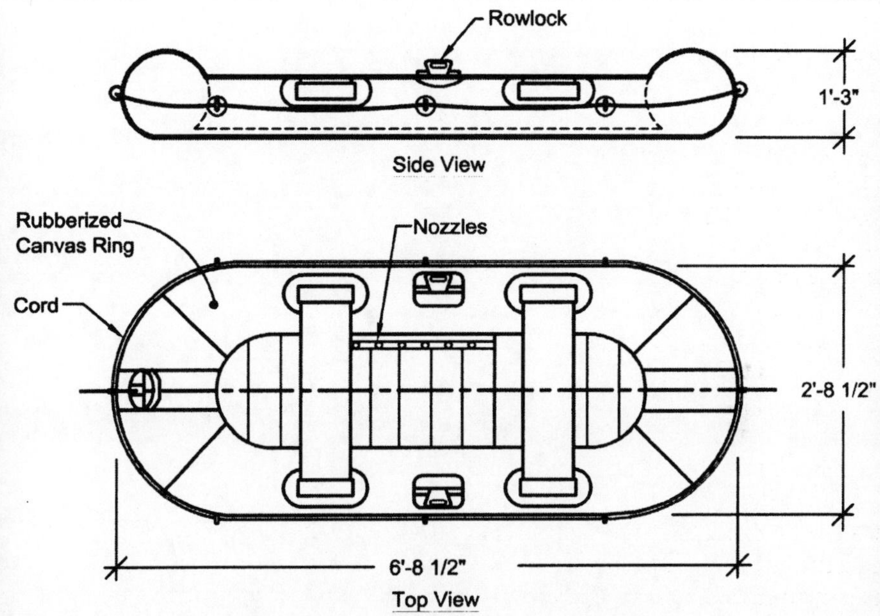

Reconnaissance Boat
(n.t.s.)

Stubborn

Captain Brown's party returned to the brigade location at 0630 on the 23rd and an hour later were greeted with very heavy shelling and mortaring. Eight men were wounded. At the Sonnenberg, the mortar fire and shell fire started at 0710 and continued heavily throughout the day. Stan Holden: *"When the shelling stopped it became unnaturally quiet and still, except for the cracking of tree branches breaking off. The ground was gradually becoming covered with these small branches falling down, cut by the shelling. During one shelling Sappers Rawling and Higgins, who were sharing a trench with Captain Cromie in the little copse, were both killed. Captain Cormie had one side of his face pitted with black bits of shrapnel; otherwise he was unhurt except for shock."* [69]

At 1315 the enemy attacked but were driven off. Shortly after, the heavy mortar fire ensued and the enemy approached to within grenade throwing distance and then retreated back into the trees. The sappers were holding fast, but their numbers were slowly dwindling as the aid stations filled.

As the sun rose on Sunday September 24th the light revealed two bodies with their heads blown off in a nearby trench. From what Stan Holden observed, it seems that the two unfortunate men were looking over when a shell had landed on the edge of their trench. Stan Holden, *"The chap at the rear had his hand on the shoulder of the man in front. The hand was scratched by shrapnel and I think the shell had landed behind them. The chap in front had only his chin left, otherwise they were both decapitated.*

The remains of a jeep somewhere on the Oranjeweg in 1945. (Geert Maassen)

There were bits of their flesh strewn about the trench. Six of us gathered around them; I remember Corporal Hyatt and Sapper Richards. Somebody suggested taking their nametags, but there were no volunteers for such a gruesome job."

Nor were there volunteers to take the bodies to the outhouse, the temporary morgue. Inside there were nine or ten bodies piled on the floor. At one point Stan Holden listened to three men who he did not know, debate whether it was ethical to look for food in their packs. He doubted if anyone had any food by this time. Stan Holden, *"By now we had almost given up hope of ever seeing the Second Army, and General Dempsey and various other top brass had been well and truly cursed. However, one good thing was that things seemed a little quieter and we were able to move about a bit easier."* [70]

A glider pilot came by with the meal for the day. It consisted of one biscuit and one boiled sweet per man. Also, word was spread that the standing order was to only fire when the enemy was seen clearly. At 1900 the enemy tried to overrun the positions, but were beaten off with casualties.

All day the reserve was subject to heavy shelling and mortaring, causing two wounded. Bill Grantham: *"Tommy Cunningham was my number two on the PIAT. We were running out of bombs and I told him to go and find some more, but just as he climbed out of the trench he was hit by gunfire. He screamed in pain and I knew he had been seriously wounded, he was taken away by the medics and that was the last I saw of Tommy."* Sadly, he didn't make it. Sapper Thomas Cunningham's Field Grave was behind Paasberg School, which was one of the aid stations.[71]

Captain Brown was ordered by the brigade to take 14 men as replacements to the 156 Para. Battalion's position, some 75 yards to the north. There he found that the battalion was only two officers and 12 men. They were told that there was no room for them and were sent back. Afterwards they were told to stand by for reinforcement role to the 21st Independent Company.

Looking west near the crossroads showing the remains of a PIAT position. Like the other photos of the area, it was taken by J. Leusden in 1945. (Geert Maassen)

Withdraw

As per usual, both positions were shelled and mortared all day on Monday September 25th. Stan Holden: *"Sometime during the day someone came around to the trenches to tell us that we would be retiring across the river during the next night. We were told not to talk about it, and also that we would be briefed on the operation later in the day. I remember feeling a little disappointed. As things had become a little quieter I didn't see the point in leaving."* [72]

Captain Brown was summoned to a brigade conference at Div HQ. There he learned that Lt-Col Murray of the Glider Pilots Regiment had assumed command of the brigade after Brig. Hackett had been seriously wounded. He also learned of General Urquhart's urgent message to Lt-Gen Browning.

Stan Holden was one of 30 odd troops at the briefing given by Captain Cormie. They were informed that the perimeter would be gradually evacuated from top to bottom and, as the squadron was mid-way down, they would leave at about 21.00 hours. The Military Police would lay white tape to guide the way and the Royal Artillery would fire tracer shells from across the river throughout the whole evacuation to mark the crossing point. The men were told to wear socks over their boots to muffle any noise, and all equipment had to be secured to prevent any clattering. *"He picked half a dozen men to be the last to leave so they could fire the odd bullet from the trenches to try to fool the Germans that we were still there. Someone asked about the Poles, but we were told not to tell them, which shows how neurotic we had become. The wounded had to be left behind in the cellar in the capable hands of the medical orderly, and would presumably be made prisoner."* [72]

The reserve vacated the positions at 2045 and moved to the river.

Captain Brown's reaction to the withdrawal orders: *"We were glum. We really felt that we had failed. We all shaved for the first time during the op, muffled our boots , stopped all jingles, and started off in a silent swaying crocodile for the river. Since I had been there and knew the way, I led what remained of the 4 Para Bde – 54 souls. We passed very silently within 100 yards of a German mortar position and eventually, guided by glider pilots at main turnings, we reached the river banks at 694769 where orderly queues of men waited their turn for the boats. And here we witnessed a very smoothly running engineer job. 43 Div. RE and some Canadian sappers were operating a quick ferry service of stormboats."* [73]

At 2215 the entire party arrived at boats and the party from the Sonnenberg arrived at the same time. Captain Cormie's party reached the river 15 minutes later and made contact with Captain Smith.

Captain Smith: *"The route down to the river had been marked out the previous night by the Glider Pilot regiment and as units we left our positions, obviously in a carefully scheduled order. We moved off in the dark in a single file as silently as possible each man holding on to the man in front and I think it was about midnight when my troop finally reached the river. Just as we got there and were waiting in line, the Germans apparently realized what was going on and laid down a heavy mortar barrage which sank several boats and making it a very unhealthy place indeed. I took my troop upstream about a couple hundred yards and stopped on one of the several stone groins that stuck out a few yards into the river. I had a small flashlight which I shielded and kept flashing at the south bank. We were getting very discouraged when we had no response for what seemed like hours and were trying to figure out whether any of us could swim across and hopefully convince a boat that our flashing light was not a German one. The river was about 150 yds wide with a fairly strong current and in the dark it looked black and about a mile wide. I used to be a fairly good swimmer but we were all cold, wet and tired and it just looked to be too much, although I learned later that some men did manage it – mostly among those who were still stranded just before first light and who had not much to loose by trying it. We didn't quite come to that point fortunately. I'm not sure how long it really was before we heard a boat chugging towards us but a Canadian sapper had finally decided to take a chance, bless his heart. By the time he arrived our numbers had increased to about double what we had to start with and it took him more than 4 trips loaded to the gunnels to get us all across but each time he did come back for more,*

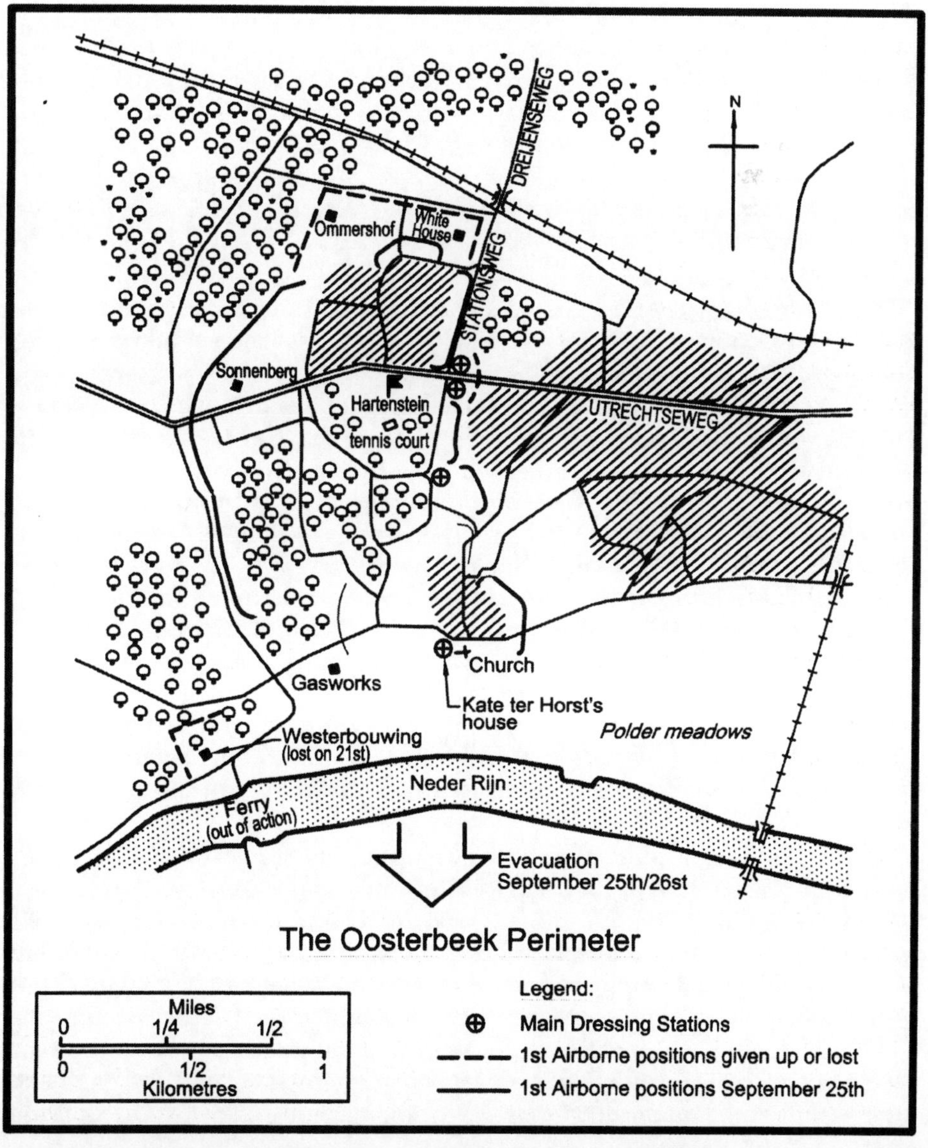

which took a lot of guts considering what was going on." [74]

The Canadian sapper was most likely R. LeBouthillier of the 23rd Field Company, R.C.E.

Captain Brown and his men found an abandoned assault boat that he figured was left behind by the Poles crossing a few nights ago and he and about fourteen other men paddled it across. His plan was to return with three men to pick up the next load. However, when they reached the south shore, they were greeted by what he describes as an enormous Canadian Engineer Officer who had other ideas. When the Captain started back to the boat , he put his large hand on the Captain's shoulder and asked him, "Where the hell are you going?" The Captain told him of the plan to go back for the rest of his men and was told that there were well rested sappers who would do the job. This officer was 6'-4" Lieutenant Bob Tate of the 23rd Field Company, R.C.E.

By 0030 the entire party crossed the river with one man wounded. Grantham: *"Eventually I got across on a boat manned by a Canadian. On the other side the climb to the top of the bank was steep and slippery. I picked up a badly wounded soldier and hoisted him across my shoulder. I cautiously made my way up to the top under intense mortar fire. I handed the wounded man over to the medics before making my way to a gathering point."* [75]

The Sonnenberg party crossed over in Assault boats manned by the 260th Field Company, R.E. At 0300, what was left of the squadron was fed and moved to Nijmegen. Captain Smith: *"Once across, we were guided down the road for about a mile where we got aboard a thing called a DUKW, sort of a boat with wheels. The country south of the river was quite different and was more like the polderland that one associates with Holland. Anyway after we had been on this thing for a few minutes it slid quietly off the road down the embankment and onto its side in the mud. About this time I think we were all about ready to burst into tears. We had been packed into this thing like sardines in a can and I assume that's why there were so few people hurt. After walking along the road for an hour or so it was starting to get light when we got a ride on a truck and were taken down the road to Nijmegen where we had a good hot meal and a speech from General Browning which maybe made him feel better but didn't do a great deal for us. We slept in a school that night and flew back to England the next day – incidentally leaving the two American Airborne Divisions behind."* [76]

Sapper Grantham remembers the overwhelming stench of the battle, the noise and concentrated gunfire of a bitter and – as he put it – *"furious battle of a unit committed to hold out to the end"* and lastly, the hunger. He stated that he was constantly hungry, wanted a cigarette badly, but strangely didn't feel exhausted until he was safely back in Nijmegen.

Not all made it across. Driver Richard Walker must have been killed sometime during the evacuation because his field grave was located on the south side of river. Stan Holden's party took a wrong turn in the dark and after stumbling around decided to give up. He and others were captured the next day. Jo Johanson: *"The days were very monotonous and I wished I was back with the boys. We were listening to the whine of bullets past the window and the shells at they exploded outside but we just had to hope for the best and wait for 2nd Army. I found others from the Squadron inside, Cardwell, Coiden, Burton, Peacock and Macintosh, they all had a story to tell. There was very little food, hardly any medicines or bandages and just the floor to lay on. On Sunday the Germans arrived, I was a bit slow going downstairs when the barrel of a Sten Gun appeared round the edge of the door which was followed by a German in a hat. Underneath it was four foot six inches of the master race, his eyes were hidden by the brim of the helmet and I felt like advising him to go to the stores for a smaller one. The gun was pointing menacingly at me, he had a pistol in his belt a rifle on his back and about fourteen grenades dangling from his waist. When he motioned for me to go downstairs I thought it better to obey him. Even so, when I turned my head away I smiled to think this specimen had me in his power, but whether he was big or small and had a pistol or an 88mm I was now a prisoner of war."* [77]

After Word

When the 4th Parachute Squadron, R.E. was first raised it was unclear of their exact role. In time this became defined; they were to support the 4th Parachute Brigade in any way they could, which was intended to be field engineering. Though they were all trained soldiers, the majority of the squadron were skilled tradesmen who were more valuable when they held tools like welding torches and wire clippers rather than guns. Yet, because of circumstances, they were called upon to support the brigade by performing the most basic function that a soldier can do, and that is to fight.

And this they did well. Once they were dug in they were a unit committed to hold out to the end, even when the fighting was bitter and furious; even when their stomachs were empty. The squadron proved that they could not be moved and two large houses, both of which are no longer standing, the Sonnenberg and the Ommershof, are a testament to the squadron's perseverance. They defended these homes despite the mounting casualties and the lack of supplies.

Of the ten officers and 147 men that landed on the 17th and 18th, only five officers and 64 men made it across the river and back into Second Army's lines to fight another day. Nineteen men were killed, with five of them without a known grave. Sixty-nine sappers were made prisoners, with the majority of them wounded.

Once back in the U.K., it was not long before the squadron merged with the 1st Parachute Squadron in order to have at least one squadron up to strength. Later they reformed with an upgraded War Establishment as the 1st Airborne Squadron, RE. This restructuring was directly the result of the lessons learned at Arnhem. The Royal Engineers in future operations, would land with far more equipment and an upgraded organization.

As a result, their firepower was increased to 17 PIATS, 20 Machine guns and 6 2" mortars.

It was not until May 1945 that the squadron had their next assignment, the liberation of Norway. It was called Operation Doomsday. The war ended before it could take place, but the plan was modified so that the division could occupy the country. Fortunately, this operation went more smoothly than the Arnhem drop and they were back in the U.K. in August. It was finally the end of a long journey that had started in the Middle East. Throughout their travels the 4th Parachute Squadron, Royal Engineers had performed every function that it was asked to, including the most basic.[78]

Notes:

1 –`Arnhem: The Airborne Battle' by Martin Middlebrook /`The History Of The Corps Of Royal Engineers Volume IX'/ `Army Commando 1940-1945' by Mike Chappell /`A Sapper At Arnhem: The Memoirs Of Harry Faulkner-Brown' by Harry Faulkner-Brown/ `Who Was Who'
2 -`British Army Of The Rhine – Operations In North West Europe' (1946) Captain Browns' account
3 -`CRE 1 Airborne Div. Op. Instruction No 1 – 12 Sept 1944' / `The History Of The Corps Of Royal Engineers Volume IX'
4 - British Army Of The Rhine – Operations In North West Europe' (1946) Major Perkins' account
5 - Account by Sapper Jo Johanson / Account Captain Brown
6 - Account by Sapper Jo Johanson
7 – Account by Sapper Jo Johanson / `It Never Snows In September' by Robert J. Kershaw page 110
8 - Account by Sapper Jo Johanson
9 –Mini Story No. 86 `The 11th Para. Bn. At Arnhem' by Niall Cherry
10–Account by Sapper Jo Johanson
11–`Arnhem 1944: The Airborne Battle' by Martin Middlebrook page 223 /`It Never Snows In September' by R. Kershaw
12-Account by Sapper Jo Johanson
13-British Army Of The Rhine – Operations In North West Europe' (1946) Major Perkins' account
14-`A Sapper At The Sonnenberg' Mini Story No. 83 by Stan Holden in the Airborne Museum Newsletter Operations In North West Europe' (1946) Major Perkins' account
15–`Roll of Honour' by J.A. Hey
16- British Army Of The Rhine – Operations In North West Europe' (1946) Captain H.F. Brown's account
17– Account by Grantham
18– Account by Weymouth
19- War Diary / Public Record Office / Steve McLaughin's website on the 4th Para. Sqn. RE /`A Sapper At The Sonnenberg' Mini Story No. 83 by Stan Holden in the Airborne Museum Newsletter / Account by Weymouth / War Diary
20- Account by Sapper Jo Johanson
21–British Army Of The Rhine – Operations In North West Europe' (1946) Major Perkins' account
22-`A Sapper At The Sonnenberg' Mini Story No. 83 by Stan Holden in the

Airborne Museum Newsletter
23–Account by Sapper Jo Johanson
24-`A Sapper At The Sonnenberg' Mini Story No. 83 by Stan Holden in the Airborne Museum Newsletter
25-`Arnhem 1944: The Airborne Battle' by Martin Middlebrook page / Account by W.C. Grantham
26-Public Record Office / Steve McLaughin's website on the 4th Para. Sqn. RE
27-`A Sapper At The Sonnenberg' Mini Story No. 83 by Stan Holden in the Airborne Museum Newsletter
28–Account by Perkins
29–Account by Captain Smith
30–McCoy / 4th Para. Squadron, R.E. War Diary September 1944
31-Public Record Office / Steve McLaughin's website on the 4th Para. Sqn. RE
32–Account by Captain Smith
33-Account by Sapper Jo Johanson
34–British Army Of The Rhine – Operations In North West Europe' (1946) Major Perkins' account
35- Account by Weymouth
36–`Arnhem 1944: The Airborne Battle' by Martin Middlebrook page 330
37-4th Para. Squadron, R.E. War Diary September 1944
38-Account by Sapper Jo Johanson/ British Army Of The Rhine – Operations In North West Europe' (1946) Major Perkins' account
39–4th Para. Squadron, R.E. War Diary September 1944 / `A Sapper At The Sonnenberg' Mini Story No. 83 by Stan Holden in the Airborne Museum Newsletter
40–Account by Captain Smith
41–Account by Sapper Jo Johanson
42-Public Record Office / Steve McLaughin's website on the 4th Para. Sqn. RE
43 - British Army Of The Rhine – Operations In North West Europe' (1946) Major Perkins' account
44–Public Record Office / Steve McLaughin's website on the 4th Para. Sqn. RE
45–British Army Of The Rhine – Operations In North West Europe' (1946) Major Perkins' account
46–`Arnhem 1944: The Airborne Battle' by Martin Middlebrook page 354
47-Public Record Office / Steve McLaughin's website on the 4th Para. Sqn. RE
48-Account by Sapper Jo Johanson
49-British Army Of The Rhine – Operations In North West Europe' (1946) Major Perkins' account
50-Public Record Office / Steve McLaughin's website on the 4th Para. Sqn. RE / 4th Para. Squadron, R.E. War Diary September 1944 /`A Sapper At The Sonnenberg' Mini Story No. 83 by Stan Holden in the Airborne Museum Newsletter
51-4th Para. Squadron, R.E. War Diary September 1944 /(10)
52-4th Para. Squadron, R.E. War Diary September 1944 / Public Record Office / Steve McLaughin's website on the 4th Para. Sqn. RE
53–Captain H.F. Brown account for `British Army Of The Rhine – Operations in North West Europe' (1946)
54–Middlebrook / 4th Para. Squadron, R.E. War Diary September 1944
55–`A Sapper At The Sonnenberg' Mini Story No. 83 by Stan Holden in the Airborne Museum Newsletter
56–`A Sapper At The Sonnenberg' Mini Story No. 83 by Stan Holden in the Airborne Museum Newsletter
57–Account by Grantham
58–Public Record Office / Steve McLaughin's website on the 4th Para. Sqn. RE
59–`A Sapper At The Sonnenberg' Mini Story No. 83 by Stan Holden in the Airborne Museum Newsletter
60–Account by Grantham
61–Account by Grantham
62–Accounts Brown/Smith 63–4th Para. Squadron, R.E. War Diary September 1944 / Account by Brown
64–`A Sapper At The Sonnenberg' Mini Story No. 83 by Stan Holden in the Airborne Museum Newsletter
65–Hyatt's MM citation / Public Record Office / Steve McLaughin's website on the 4th Para. Sqn. RE
66–Account by Sapper Jo Johanson
67–`A Sapper At The Sonnenberg' Mini Story No. 83 by Stan Holden in the Airborne Museum Newsletter
68–Account by Captain Brown
69–`A Sapper At The Sonnenberg' Mini Story No. 83 by Stan Holden in the Airborne Museum Newsletter
70-`A Sapper At The Sonnenberg' Mini Story No. 83 by Stan Holden in the Airborne Museum Newsletter
71–Grantham / Roll of Honour
72–`A Sapper At The Sonnenberg' Mini Story No. 83 by Stan Holden in the Airborne Museum Newsletter
73- Captain H.F. Brown account for `British Army Of The Rhine – Operations in North West Europe' (1946)
74–Account by Smith
75–Account by Grantham
76-Account by Captain Smith
77–Account by Sapper Jo Johanson / Roll of Honour
78-`Lessons From Arnhem' / War Diary / `British Army W.E. Tables N.W. Europe June 44/ May 45' by Gary Kennedy

Roll Of Honour

Captain Nigel B. Beaumont-Thomas
93266; age 28. Killed on September 20th and buried in Oosterbeek.

Lieutenant Michael C. Eden
267948; age 22. Killed on September 21st and buried in Oosterbeek.

Corporal John B. Cooper
2122170; age 29. Date of death is unclear and has no known grave.

Corporal Reginald F Talyor
1895265; age 25. Date of death is unclear and has no known grave.

Lance Corporal Leo J. Ackland
1579023; age 25. Killed on September 20th and buried in Oosterbeek.

Lance Corporal William Ball
1877136; age 23. Died on September 29th and is buried in Oosterbeek.

Lance Corporal Charles E Salmon
4747388; age 23. Killed on September 20th and buried in Oosterbeek.

Sapper Richard L. Adderley
3530704; age 19. Killed on September 20th and is buried in Oosterbeek.

Sapper Thomas Cunningham
2070187; age 30. Killed on September 24th and is buried in Oosterbeek.

Sapper Philip S. Epps
14638749; age 19. Killed on September 19th and is buried in Oosterbeek.

Sapper Bernard Higgins
2074226; age 22. Killed on September 23rd and is buried in Oosterbeek.

Sapper Geoffrey F.W. Morrison
2002918; age 27. Killed on September 20th and has no known grave.

Sapper Leonard D. Rawlings
1949495; age 23. Killed on September 23rd and is buried in Oosterbeek.

Sapper Harry Smith
unknown; unknown; Died of Wounds in October.

Sapper Reginald Willers
14511180; age 20. Killed on September 22nd and is buried in Oosterbeek.

Sapper Roderick J. Williams
4205196; age 22. Killed on September 21st and has no known grave.

Sapper Frederik Yates
2117843; age 24. Killed on September 20th and has no known grave.

Driver Dennis Seabrook
5958824; age 22. Killed on September 26th and is buried in Oosterbeek.

Driver Richard Walker
14433016; age 20. Killed during the withdrawal and is buried in Oosterbeek.

Nominal Roll

Went in: 157 men / Died:19 / Evac: 64 / Missing: 74
(* best guess / Evac=Evacuated / W=wounded/ ^ unlikely)

Advance Party: Chalk# 144

Lt. Evans	W/POW
L/Cpl Johanson	W/POW
Spr. O'Donnell	W/POW

Motor Transport:
Gliders 965 to 967:

Lt. Eden	KIA
L/Sgt.H.L. Gordon	W/POW
L/Cpl Alan Aldcroft	W/POW
Spr. Ken Coley	W/POW
Spr. Don Stevens	W/POW
Spr. Philip Epps	KIA
Eric McCoy	Evac
Dvr. Stan Bower	W/POW
Dvr. A. Wheeler	POW
Spr. A. Bailey*	Evac
Spr. Fox*	Evac
Spr. J. Storie*	unknown

Attached: Glider #968

Lt. Skinner	Murdered
L/Cpl. Roff	POW
L/Cpl. Trim	POW
Spr. Connolly	POW
Dvr. Day	POW
Dvr. Whitmore	POW

Chalk 718 – 1st Troop

Captain J.C.A. Smith	Evac
L/Sgt. J.E. Robinson	W/POW
Cpl. M.C. Flannery	W/POW
Cpl. A.W. Stringwell	Evac
L/Cpl. J.P. Hodkinson	W/POW
Spr. G.F. Cratchley	W/POW
Spr. G.C. Cook	W/POW
Spr. Tom Cunningham	KIA
Spr. A. Parker	Evac
Spr. R.E. Phillips	W/POW
Spr. M. Plumridge	W/POW
Spr. D.S. Randle	W/POW
Spr. R. Sands	Evac
Spr. W.K. Sharp	Evac
Pte. M. Skelly	W/POW
Dvr. D. Seabrook	KIA

Chalk 719 – 1st Troop

Sgt. D. McCutchloon	W/POW
Cpl. R.J. Holland	Evac
L/Cpl. R. Shaw	Evac
L/Cpl. R. Laidler	W/POW
L/Cpl. L.J. Ackland	KIA
Spr. W. Ankers	Evac
Spr. H. Arnold	Evac
Spr. F. Baines	Evac
Spr. A. Burton	W/POW
Spr. J. Creighton	Evac
Spr. A.R.C. Horton	Evac
Spr. C. Nealon	Evac
Spr. R. Paterson	W/POW
Spr. J. Reid	W/POW
Spr. T. Simpson	Evac
Spr. J.S.H. Phillips	W/POW

Chalk 720 – Mixed

Captain N.B. Thomas	KIA
Cpl. F. Smithyos	W/POW
L/Cpl. H. Howard	W/POW
Spr. E.A. Cardwell	W/POW
Spr. W.C. Grantham	Evac
Spr. F.W. Peacook	W/POW
Spr. J. Plested	Evac
Cpl. S.S. Tennant	Evac
Spr. H. Goldsmith	Evac
Spr. L. Hanlon	Evac
Spr. J. Parish	Evac
Spr. I. Sherrand	Evac
Spr. V. Whittle	W/POW
Spr. F. Yates	KIA
Dvr. R. Walker	KIA

Chalk 721 – 2 Troop

Capt. J.J. McCormie	unknown
Sgt. R. McGowan	W/POW
L/Cpl. H. Quinn	W/POW
L/Cpl. W. Ball	Died Wounds
L/Cpl. A.S. Combey	W/POW
Spr. R. Beardsley	Evac
Spr. J. Dalton	Evac
Spr. E.V. Capper	W/POW
Spr. V.G. Gilchrist	W/POW
Spr. W.A. Coulsting	Evac
Spr. H. Hearn	Evac
Spr. W.T.F. Higgins	Evac
Spr. T.W. Miller	W/POW
Spr. R.F. Skidmore	W/POW
Spr. H. Smith	Died Wounds
Dvr. A. Davies	Evac

Chalk 722 – 2 Troop

2Lt. K.A. Hall	Evac
Spr. W.T. Mckenna	W/POW
Spr. R. Willers	KIA
L/Sgt. T.R.F. McGrath	Evac
Cpl. G. Hopkins	Evac
L/Cpl. R. Hodgson	Evac
L/Cpl. A.W. Bradley	W/POW
L/Cpl. W. Cranfield	W/POW
Spr. K. Allsop	Evac
Spr. J.J. Ellard	W/POW
Spr. B. Higgins	KIA
Spr. G. Mackay	Evac
Spr. H. McLean	Evac
Spr. L.D. Rawlings	KIA
Spr. A.E. Spooner	W/POW
Spr. R.J. Wallace	Evac

Chalk 723 – HQ

Major A.J.M. Perkins	W/POW
W.O.II E.S.J. Marriott	WPOW
Cpl. I.J.L. Lewis	W/POW
Spr. G.F.W. Morrison	KIA
Spr. C. Playle *	W/POW
Spr. E.P. Ratcliffe	Evac
Spr. J. Standen	Evac
Spr. T.K. Stott	Evac
Spr. D.H. Dorkin	W/POW
Spr. D.W. Barber	Evac
L/Sgt N.A. Keeler	W/POW
Cpl. C.V. Kelly	Evac
Spr. N. Benzie	W/POW
Spr. G. Denholm	Evac
Spr. R.H. Smith	Evac
Spr. J. Partridge	Evac

Chalk 724 – 3rd Troop

Lt. N.L.B. Thomas	Evac
L/Sgt. E. Greenwood	Evac
Cpl. C.R. Comerford	W/POW
L/Cpl. G. Blyth	Evac
L/Cpl. C.E. Salmon	KIA
Spr. A.E. Ayers	POW
Spr. J.E. Bromilow	W/POW
Spr. N. Cook	Evac
Spr. S. Holden	W/POW
Spr. C.F. Mackintosh	W/POW
Spr. T.B. Paterson	W/POW
Spr. R.F. Ross	W/POW
Spr. I. Saul	Evac
Spr. P. Weldon	W/POW
Spr. J.H. Wilson	Evac
Spr. H. Hulse	Evac

Chalk 725 – 3rd Troop

Capt. H.F. Brown	Evac
Sgt. P.R.W. Martin	W/Evac
Cpl. J.B. Cooper	KIA
L/Cpl. D.R. Morris	Evac
Spr. R.L. Adderley	KIA
Spr. H. Beaumont	Evac
Spr. J. Cash	W/POW
Spr. N.G. Coleman	Evac
Spr. L. Gordon	W/POW
Spr. A.W. Guanlet	W/POW
Spr. W. Horsman	Evac
Spr. P Hyatt MM	Evac
Spr. W. Watson	Evac
Spr. R.J. Williams	KIA
Spr. E. Worthington	Evac
Spr. W.H. Williams	W/POW

Chalk 726 – 3rd Troop

Lt. G.S. Harris -	W/POW
L/Cpl M.V. Weymouth	POW
Spr. H.S.A. Coles	W/POW
Dvr. J. Scarfe	W/POW
Dvr. R. Alsop	Evac
Cpl. R.F. Taylor	KIA
Spr. J. O'Donnell^	W/POW
Spr. W. Bull	Evac
Spr. E. Richards	W/POW
Spr. DGA Coilden	W/POW
Spr. T. Turner	W/POW
Spr. Jack Leonard	Evac
Spr A.H. Scott	Evac
L/Cpl Cyril Brown	Evac
Spr. George Winnett	Evac

References:

Primary Sources:

Major A.E.J.M. Perkins account for `British Army Of The Rhine – Operations in North West Europe' (1946)
Captain (Major) H.F. Brown account for `British Army Of The Rhine – Operations in North West Europe' (1946)
Account: Captain Smith
Mini Story No. 83 by Stan Holden in the Airborne Museum Newsletter
Account by Jo Johanson in a letter to Philip Reinders
Ryan Archive
Account `Arnhem And After' by Maurice V. Weymouth
Account by W.C. Grantham in a letter to Philip Reinders
Citation: Sapper P. Hyatt
War Diary: 4th Para. Sqn. RE Sept. 1944
CRE 1 Airborne Division Op. Instruction No. 1 12 Sept 1944

Secondary Sources:

`The History Of The Corps Of Royal Engineers Vol. IX'
`Royal Engineers Battlefield Tour: The Seine To The Rhine: Vol.1' Feb 1947
`A Bridge Too Far' by C. Ryan
`Poles Apart' by George Cholewczynski
`Then And Now Operation Market Garden' by Karl Margry
`Reconstitution of the British Airborne Division' by Philip Reinders
`The 4th Para. Brigade HQ During The Battle Of Arnhem Sept. 1944' by Philip Reinders
`Hell's Highway' by Tim Saunders
`Arnhem 1944: The Airborne Battle' by Martin Middlebrook
`Roll Of Honour Battle of Arnhem 17-26 Sept 44' by J.A. Hey
`Airborne Engineers: The Shiny 9th' by Patrick Pronk
Mini Story No. 86 by Naill Cherry in the Airborne Museum Newsletter
`A Sapper At Arnhem: The Memoirs of Harry Faulkner Brown' by Harry Faulkner Brown
Steve McLaughin's website on the 4th Para. Sqn. RE
`British Airborne Troops' by Barry Gregory
`The Royal Air Force At Arnhem: Glider and Resupply missions in Sept. 44' by L Buist, P. Reinder, G. Maasen
`C-47/R4D Units of the ETO and MTO' by David Isby
`Who Was Who During The Battle of Arnhem' C. van Rockel
`A Tour of The Arnhem Battlefields' by John Waddy
`Army Commandos 1940-1943' by Mike Chappell

Index

About The Author

John Sliz became fascinated with Operation Market Garden after he read, `A Bridge Too Far' at the age of nine. A visit to Arnhem in the summer of 2001 only added fuel to the fire, eventually resulting in the publication of his first book, `The Storm Boat Kings'. While researching this book and waiting for its publication, he wrote a small booklet on the engineer equipment that was used during the operation. `Engineer Assault Boats In Canadian Service' was published in December 2006.

Another by-product of his research was an interest in engineers and this led to a small booklet on the Polish Engineer Company called, `The Wrong Side Of The River'. The first two runs have been sold out, but a second edition is in the works. This edition will be part of the Market Garden Engineer Series and, like the other books in the series, will be heavily laden with original drawings and maps. His day job as a design draftsman is put to good use.

Another book in the series, `Assault Boats On the Waal' was released in January 2010 and studies the accomplishments of the engineers of the U.S. 82nd Airborne Division during Operation Market Garden; in particularly, the bloody crossing of the Waal River where each man was pushed to the limit.

He is currently working on the other four books in this series, each studying an engineer unit during the operation.

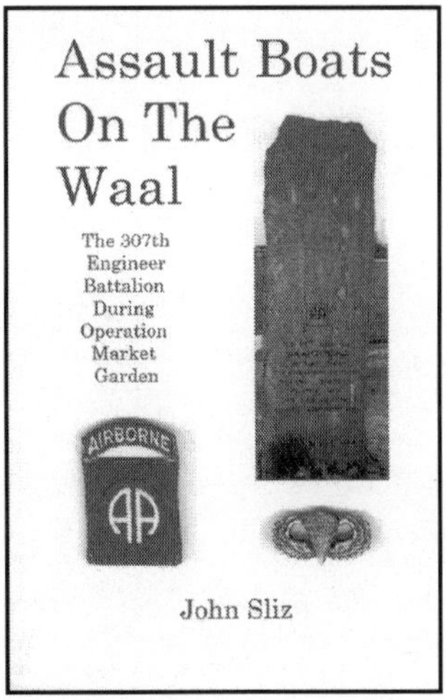

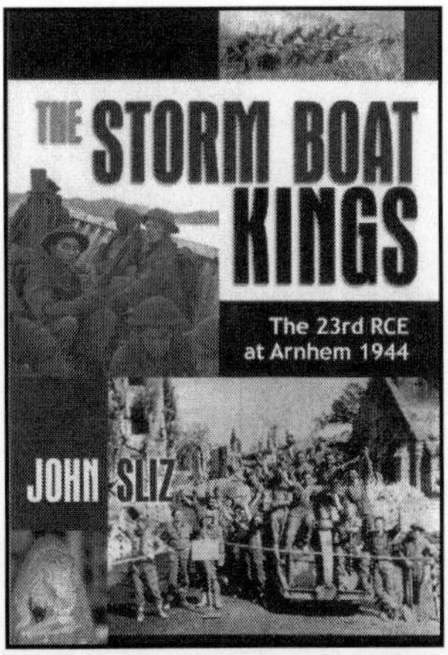

17228077R00035

Printed in Great Britain
by Amazon